6 Driving the car 108

7 Going racing 128

8 How to design and build a track 146

Appendices

Appendix 1 156

Appendix 2 170

Appendix 3 172

Appendix 4 174

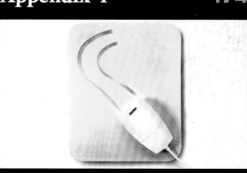

Index 175

D1712698

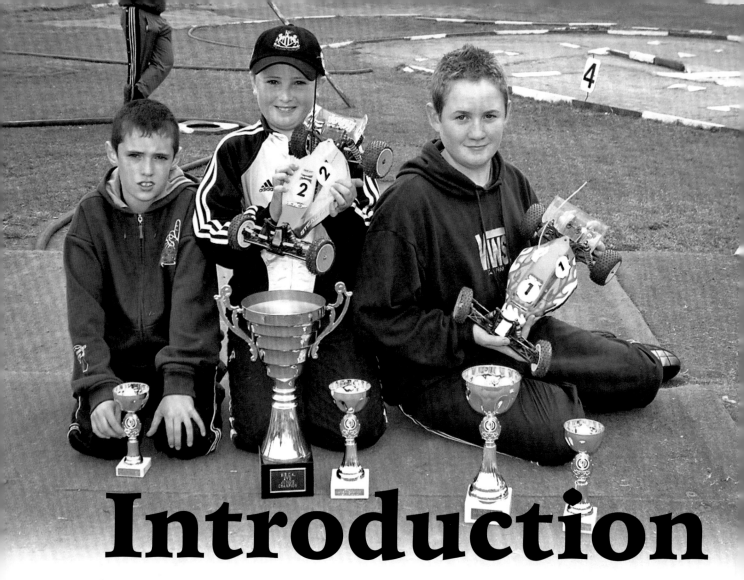

Introduction

Defining the hobby – what radio control is all about . . .

So what is a radio control (RC) model car? For the majority of people, the term conjures up images of the vast array of toys sold in High Street toyshops. Often characterised by dismal battery life and disappointing performance, these toy cars tend to leave a poor impression that lasts a lot longer than the cars themselves. Many such gleaming Christmas presents have had to be thrown away on Boxing Day along with the packaging, as unsuspecting owners find out the hard way that their new toy can't be repaired after it's crashed into the fireplace or the Christmas tree and suffered a broken suspension arm or wheel.

If you haven't experienced a true RC model, then please don't compare the two! Despite sharing the conceptual similarity of being controlled via a hand-held transmitter, these radio control toys have virtually nothing in common with a true RC model car, and comparing the two is like comparing a paper aeroplane with a supersonic jet fighter. Modern RC cars are high-performance, technical pieces of equipment that should be compared to full-size motor sport examples. Whether your passion for motor sport lies in Formula One, touring cars or monster trucks, there's an RC kit available that will allow you to drive your scale replica to the limit, without fear of hurting yourself. And it won't cost a fortune. With performance that can achieve speeds in excess of 70mph, shock absorbers that are adjustable for static and compression damping, ride height and spring rates, you can buy an RC model with a carbon fibre chassis, titanium nitride shock shafts and aluminium components straight off the retailer's shelf.

LEFT The radio control hobby appeals to all ages and can be enjoyed by parents as much as their youngsters! Mums and dads are often an important part of racing.

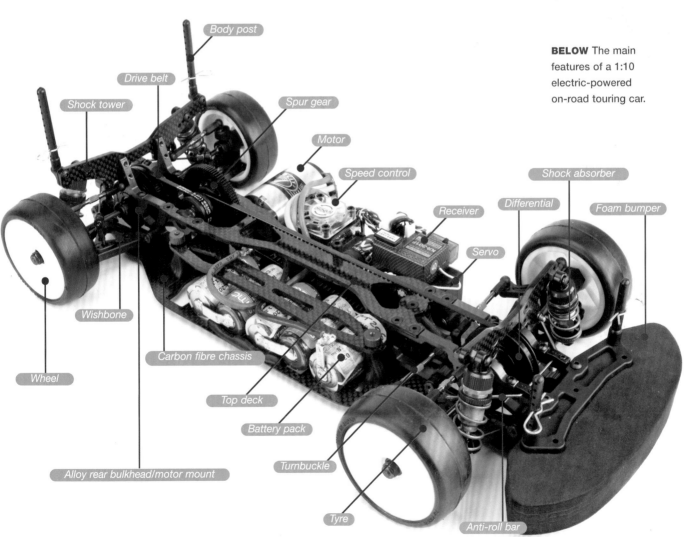

BELOW The main features of a 1:10 electric-powered on-road touring car.

Body post

Drive belt

Shock tower

Spur gear

Motor

Speed control

Shock absorber

Receiver

Differential

Foam bumper

Servo

Wishbone

Carbon fibre chassis

Wheel

Top deck

Battery pack

Alloy rear bulkhead/motor mount

Turnbuckle

Tyre

Anti-roll bar

RIGHT The main features of a 1:8 nitro-powered off-road truck.

Splash guard

Radio tray

Air filter

Engine

Centre driveshaft

Chassis brace

Rear wing

Alloy shock tower

Front gearbox

Bumper

Threaded shock absorber body

Tyre

Side guard

Fuel tank

Clutch

Exhaust and manifold

Alloy chassis

ABOVE Modern-day electric RC kits like this four-wheel drive touring car are packed with the latest technology, as this picture shows. With its carbon fibre chassis, titanium pivot pins and anodised alloy components, you're looking at an uncomproming piece of equipment.

LEFT With their high-performance and incredible strength, nitro-powered buggies and truggies are two of the most popular forms of RC today. *(Adrian Svensson)*

BELOW The kit in the foreground is 1:5 scale and is powered by a 22cc two-stroke petrol engine. As it races alongside a full-size Baja buggy you can see where it got its design cues from. *(Xtreme RC Cars Magazine)*

RIGHT Although building and preparing an RC model can give you great pleasure, it's when you get to drive it that you can really have some fun and test out the awesome handling. *(Adrian Svensson)*

BELOW This is a ready-to-run model and consequently comes with everything you see here. With the body already painted and the radio equipment installed, an RTR model is quicker and easier to get up and running.

For some, controlling a dynamic moving object through the wonder of radio waves is something they simply can't wait to do, whilst for others much of the thrill comes from the miniature engineering and assembly of the model.

Whatever your fancy, there's a radio control model car for you. With the latest ready-to-run (RTR) models, buyers are only a matter of minutes away from their first real RC experience, as they can be run straight out of the box with virtually no additional equipment other than some fuel or AA batteries for the transmitter. If, on the other hand, the idea of assembling your car from components appeals more, then there's a large selection of kit models for you to choose from.

Building and maintaining an RC model will not only teach you engineering skills but will help you learn about mechanics and vehicle dynamics, which will in turn assist you in everyday decision making and problem solving. Driving an RC car will hone your hand-eye co-ordination and get you out of the house and into the fresh air. It's a perfect way to meet like-minded people, make new friends and develop skills like car set-up. Whether you want to race or not, there's a multitude of RC applications that you can enjoy. Most of the models available offer a good balance of performance and operating time whether powered by fuel or a battery. So if your appetite has been whetted, then read on: this book will tell you everything you need to know about RC cars.

LEFT Whilst building or maintaining an RC kit you get to learn about the mechanics, and you can utilise your skills to help improve its performance.

BELOW Get out there and have some fun. Racing an RC car provides an opportunity to meet like-minded people and test your car and skills against theirs.
(www.oople.com)

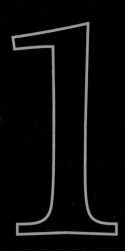

History

How radio control has developed
since its inception   14

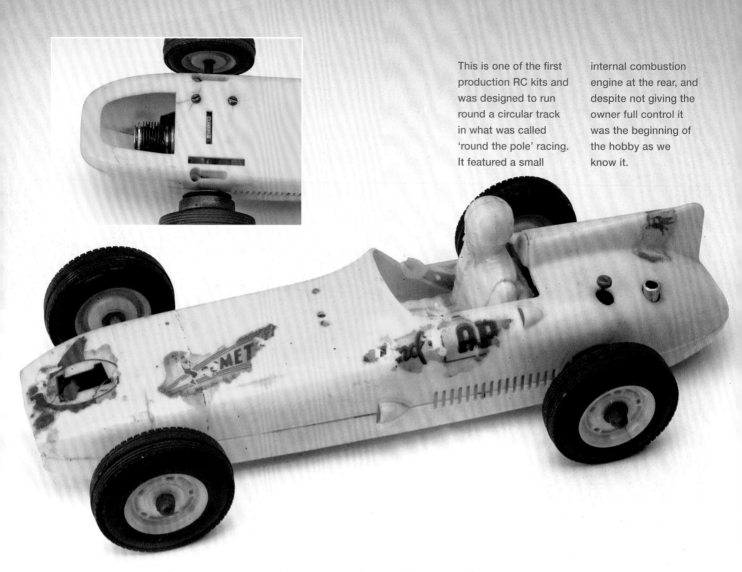

This is one of the first production RC kits and was designed to run round a circular track in what was called 'round the pole' racing. It featured a small internal combustion engine at the rear, and despite not giving the owner full control it was the beginning of the hobby as we know it.

How radio control has developed since its inception

The earliest form of radio control dates back to the 1970s, when the first true 1:8 scale nitro-powered models appeared and the racing side of the sport developed. Before this the only forms of model car competition involved slot-racing, where the only control the driver had was on the throttle; and pole-racing, where the cars were attached by a cord and raced round a circular track. These early examples, though, didn't grab the attention of the buying public, since they did little to replicate the full-size touring cars and Formula One machinery racing round the tracks of Europe and the rest of the world.

It was only with the arrival of truly proportional throttle and steering in the 1970s, allowing the cars to manoeuvre around a laid-out track, that things really took off. These 1:8 internal combustion on-road cars, though, were scratch-built, made by enthusiasts from whatever parts they could lay their hands on. Consequently they were very unreliable, and things didn't improve until cars started to be properly manufactured and the industry began to grow. Momentum really began to gain pace in the mid-1970s, by which time dedicated RC manufacturers had become established, some countries had formed national organisations to set the rules for car construction, and the first controlled race meetings had begun.

One of the first major races took place in 1978 at Monaco, where the cars raced around a temporary track laid out next to the beautiful harbour. This was won by UK driver Phil Booth, who is still involved in the hobby today.

ABOVE LEFT An example of a 1:8 on-road car from the mid-1970s.

ABOVE The cars from this period utilised engines from the model aero scene with handmade heatsinks and machined alloy rims.

LEFT The famous 1978 race meeting next to the harbour in Monaco. Note the simplicity of the track due to the limited space available.

LEFT From left to right: Phil Booth, Ted Longshaw and Dave Preston work on their cars in sunny Monaco.

RIGHT Ted Longshaw gets his car ready for racing in 1975.

BELOW This photo was taken at the Paris Grand Prix in 1975, where Ted and other members of the PB Racing Team competed against other Europeans.

TOP RIGHT The international racing scene soon developed from those in which Ted took part in the early '70s, where getting a car to run for over three minutes was a true achievement.

From these 1:8 on-road cars powered by engines, the hobby and sport took off in another direction during the following decade, when electric power became a user-friendlier alternative. The first of these electric cars were 1:10 off-road buggies, which soon gained popularity as they were much easier to understand and were assisted greatly by the advances made in batteries. Also, with their reduced noise level and ability to run on all types of surface, they could be

raced in back gardens without fear of disturbing the neighbours.

As the products improved, so did the hobby's competition side. One of the forefathers of the UK competition market was Ted Longshaw, who had first tasted radio control during a trip to the United States. His love of the sport as a racer soon led to Ted and some other now famous names setting up international race meetings so that the best UK and European drivers could compete

RIGHT The 'C' car was Schumacher's first RC car release in 1982. Designed by Englishman Cecil Schumacher, this 1:12 on-road car complete with its revolutionary ball-type differential went on to dominate the racing category, winning the European Championship in 1985 and 1988.
(Schumacher Racing)

The Hotshot from Tamiya was one of the first 4WD electric chassis and has become an off-road icon. It was the vehicle many enthusiasts purchased to start racing with.

against the rest of the world. Official World Championship events were soon in place, which attracted the top drivers to compete at venues such as Geneva, Sydney and Las Vegas. The sport had become firmly established on a global scale.

Not only did the sport grow apace, but the reliability and quality of the cars got steadily better each year as the industry went from strength to strength. As well as getting faster they also

became more technically advanced as each manufacturer tried to gain an advantage over the competition. When controlling the power started to become a problem four-wheel drive was introduced, making the cars easier to operate and utilising the available power better.

By the 1990s internal combustion-powered 1:8 on-road cars were able to achieve speeds of around 70mph, but their place at the top of the popularity charts had been taken over by the 1:10

BELOW LEFT
One-eighth on-road cars are capable of over 70mph.

BELOW A Tamiya 1:10 DTM touring car replica.

ABOVE An example of a modern-day touring chassis that features a high-quality carbon fibre chassis and alloy suspension components.

RIGHT 1:5 scale kits are the biggest in terms of size and utilise a 22cc two-stroke engine just like you'd find in something like a petrol strimmer.

OPPOSITE BOTTOM The range of ready-to-run kits is rapidly expanding and you can buy all sorts of different styles of model, including this one from Hot Bodies that comes with the radio equipment and engine installed by the factory.

cars, which replicated the full-size versions seen competing in such national and international events as the British Touring Car Championship and the German Touring Car Masters. They looked the part and handled well, and despite their touring car bodies could still achieve impressive speeds of around 40mph.

Radio control cars have come a long way in the past 30 years, and this is reflected in the public's perception of the hobby and the fact that you now regularly see them on TV programmes and in prime-time full-size car advertisements. You can also purchase an RC car in the High Street, and not necessarily from a model

shop – a true sign of how popular the product has become.

And that car won't only demonstrate tremendous quality and performance – its design will be second only to a genuine Formula One car, and will have been achieved using the latest CAD/CAM computer systems. There's also a huge range of cars, trucks and buggies to choose from, and at a price that's lower than ever – which means that there's a greater opportunity for more people to get involved and from a younger age.

Products available range from tiny 1:36 scale electric cars to huge 1:5 scale two-stroke petrol-powered machines. Not only is there a wide choice when it comes to type, but there have been considerable developments in the factory-built market, referred to as RTR or 'ready-to-run'. If you don't want to get involved in the construction of a model, most manufacturers can now offer you a ready-built version that requires just a little work to get you up and running, and these packages often work out cheaper than buying all the included items separately.

That said, you can make the hobby as competitive and professional, or as serious and expensive, as you like. Most people start out looking upon it as being a bit of fun, but it can soon become more, and if you put in the hard work and have some skill there's no reason why you can't end up travelling the world and competing against

the best that other countries have to offer. And even if that's not the case, you can still have lots of fun thrashing your RC car round the back garden, up the park with a couple of mates, or down at the local track, seeing if the new set-up you've been working on is faster. If you're interested in getting involved in RC, then this is the time to start.

ABOVE One of the smallest forms of RC, this tiny 1:36 scale Micro-T from Losi comes pre-built and is perfect for home use.

Types of RC car

Radio control over remote control **22**

Shop visit **23**

Race or recreational use? **25**

Off-road or on-road? **27**

What scale? **29**

RTR versus kit **31**

Radio control over remote control

Choosing a radio control car can be quite daunting. First of all, there are certain cars that fall into the toy category and are normally sold in toyshops, which offer little or no technical support. True RC cars, on the other hand, are typically sold by specialist retailers who can support and advise you, enhancing your experience by offering expertise and advice pertaining to the type of car you plan to purchase and the use you have in mind for it.

The first clue that what you're looking at is a toy is when it's advertised or referred to as being 'remote control'. A 'remote control' is the kind of device that allows you to change the channel on your television set, and not something that will give you full control of a model car. The name 'radio control' is applied to such models because they operate on a frequency of 27MHz, 40MHz or 2.4GHz rather than on infrared like your TV control. Other examples to avoid, for obvious reasons, are cars that are connected to the transmitter by means of a wire or lead. Although these may allow the cars to operate forwards, backwards, left and right, they're incredibly limited, and like remote control cars they generally tend to be found in toyshops. They should be avoided at all costs.

A true radio control car has enormous advantages over such inadequate models, which may be noticeably cheaper but are inferior in quality and will often break more easily, when, due to their design and method of manufacture, they normally

ABOVE Close racing is guaranteed, especially with touring cars that can rub door handles as they go side-by-side in the corners. Each car has a different paint scheme so that the drivers can identify their own at a distance.

have to be thrown away. The sellers of such items lack the technical knowledge to make repairs, and failed components can't often be replaced, so it's unsurprising that buyers who've owned such cars tend to walk away from the hobby feeling very disillusioned.

True RC cars, by contrast, can be maintained and repaired should something break, and you can also improve the way they work by upgrading parts, changing tyres and altering the set-up. Their look is easily changed too, with alternative bodyshell designs that can be sprayed in your own colours to

your own design. But one of the most notable benefits of a genuine radio control model over a toy one is that the performance is simply like comparing chalk and cheese. Any model car designed for use indoors is never going to be able to compete with a specialist product that'll test your skills for longer than just a few minutes! With this in mind, we can now take a clearer look at what's on offer and how to choose the model that's right for you.

Even with all the toys eliminated, with so many kits on the market the choice can still be tricky. A variety of different sizes, designs, methods of

ABOVE LEFT This is the latest top-of-the-range computerised transmitter from KO Propo. With a whole host of functions to suit the racer, this Esprit III Universe is feature packed.

ABOVE Maintaining your RC model is part and parcel of the hobby. During this process you'll learn more about the engineering of the car and how to look after it.

LEFT There's a massive choice in RC in terms of scale. Just look at the difference between these two Losi kits. The model at the rear is a nitro-powered 1:8 scale while the one at the front is a 1:18 electric model.

ABOVE There are many opportunities to go racing both nationally and internationally.

BELOW You don't have to go to a track to have fun. *(www.oople.com)*

propulsion and price ranges makes the initial choice seem very daunting to the uninitiated, and it can be too easy to be misled or to make an uninformed decision that results in choosing an unsuitable car for the type of use you have in mind.

This means that you'll need to carry out quality research using all the various avenues of enquiry available to you, including your local model shop, specialist magazines and the internet. The first

decision to be made is a tough one. Do you want to compete with your car, or are you simply interested in running it around the local park or your back garden? It's often a tough decision to make because at the time of making it, you may not be aware of the depth and breadth of competition available locally; and although initially you'll probably have little desire to compete, many people find the sheer thrill of competition and driving their cars round proper race tracks irresistible once tried. That said, the majority of RC car sales today are to people who'll never go anywhere near a race track and will get more than enough satisfaction and fun from blasting round with their mates! So if you fall into the fun category that makes your choice much simpler, as certain RC models are designed purely for racing.

Shop visit

The best place to see what radio control has to offer is your local model shop. If you're new to RC, a model shop will prove your main source of information and advice, as well as your first port of call for purchases. A good local retailer will allow you to check out the latest machinery, see what the

different cars have to offer, and maybe try some of the equipment for size and feel. It can also advise you about local clubs and race circuits and give you contact details so that you can talk to other people before you make decisions. You'll probably end up visiting your local shop regularly, to buy spares and new parts and to find out what's happening in your area. Details of such specialist retailers can be found in RC dedicated magazines and on the internet.

Race or recreational use?

If you decide that your car's primary usage will be purely recreational, then the decision process will inevitably centre round where you'll run it. This is because models with internal combustion (IC) engines – often referred to as nitro-powered due to the fuel that they use – may have limitations. (It's worth explaining here that although nitro-powered models use fuel it's not regular petrol, so they shouldn't be confused with petrol-powered examples.) Nitro-powered models make a lot more noise than electric-powered cars, so if you intend

to run yours in the back garden or at the local park, and don't want to upset the neighbours to the point where you're limited in the times you can use it, an electric model may be the way to go. However, if you have access to some other suitable area, such as a large unoccupied car park or an area of unused waste ground, a nitro car can be added to your list of options.

Nitro-powered models are the noisiest, smelliest,

ABOVE Get down to your local model shop, where you can see a range of kits and get the opportunity to ask the retailer all those questions you may have.

LEFT Nitro fuel is mixed for use in RC engines and can only be purchased from a specialist model shop.

RIGHT The nitro classes offer greater track time when it comes to racing. With lots of noise and power, they're also very exciting to watch.

BELOW Electric-powered models have the added benefit that they can be raced indoors.

and in 1:8 form the fastest RC cars available. For sheer excitement they can't be beaten, and just starting up a nitro-powered model will attract attention to what you're doing! But the high rpm of a nitro engine is so loud that it inevitably results in practical limitations, especially if a group of you are messing around with your cars together. As a result you'll probably need to either find an out of the way venue or else head to a local club that's tucked away in the countryside.

Compared to nitro, electric cars are quiet and clean, which means that you can run them indoors and outdoors, and as they come in a range of applications they can be run literally anywhere, from lounges to large tracks and everything in between.

Despite not having a top speed to match a high-performance nitro-powered car, 1:10 scale electric cars can be faster round a track due to their light weight and nimbleness. For example, on a tight track an electric touring car weighs-in much lighter than an equivalent nitro racer, so while it may lose out on the straights in terms of top speed, its agility and acceleration allow it to claw that time back in the twisty sections.

Off-road or on-road?

This is another choice you'll need to make. Off-road models offer the advantage of being able to race almost anywhere, and with large, long shock absorbers and knobbly tyres these vehicles can handle loose surfaces and fly through the air off big jumps. Electric 1:10 scale off-road cars are available in either two-wheel-drive (2WD) or four-wheel-drive (4WD) formats, whilst their larger 1:8 nitro cousins are nearly all 4WD. Off-road vehicles come in a range of designs which includes buggies, trucks, monster trucks and, most recently, truggies – a term, derived by combining 'buggies' and 'trucks', used to describe 1:8 nitro-powered race trucks. The range of 4WD trucks is often the most attractive to the public, with their large presence and their ability to tackle the roughest of surfaces on their chunky rubber tyres.

Unlike the off-road buggies that bear only a passing resemblance to the Baja buggies that are raced in the deserts of the United States, all on-road RC models are derived from the full-size cars that you can see racing around tracks such as

ABOVE Off-road versus on-road. The choice is yours.

LEFT An example of a 2WD buggy with its rear-mounted geared transmission and motor, with the cells down the centreline of the chassis.

BOTTOM LEFT This 4WD buggy has a forward-mounted motor and a battery pack split around the belt drive transmission.

BOTTOM RIGHT Although not that common, some monster trucks feature two engines for greater power.

ABOVE Here you can see where the HPI Baja 5B gets its looks from. *(Xtreme RC Cars Magazine)*

ABOVE RIGHT Touring cars are based on a 4WD transmission clothed in a Lexan bodyshell.

Brands Hatch and Silverstone every weekend. These touring car bodied models are much easier to identify with than the off-roaders, since unless you know anything about Baja buggies it's hard for a newcomer to relate to their design. But we see full-size versions of the on-road models every day, either in traffic or on our TV screens, participating in events such as the British Touring Car Championship. So it's no wonder that this class is one of the strongest in the RC hobby. With a

choice of 2WD and 4WD formats, on-road models can reach very high speeds, but require a smooth surface such as tarmac, concrete or carpet to race on.

With their raised suspension and deeply treaded tyres, rally car designs are tweaked from on-road chassis to allow them to run on rougher surfaces. Their off-road ability isn't as great as a purpose-built buggy or truck, but they can still handle small jumps and the like.

Going racing

Any local model shop is the perfect place to start if racing is your aim. They're often involved in racing in the vicinity, and may have links with the local club such as offering some form of support for its members; they take a healthy interest in what's going on at the local tracks and can often be the

hub for what's going on and where. If you're unfortunate and find your model shop lacks such information, the internet will provide you with an abundance of it, especially if you visit the home of the national association (BRCA) – see Appendix 2. There you'll find details of all the affiliated clubs and you should be able to quickly locate a track close to you. When you've found one, phone up and make arrangements to go along to one of their race days.

Visiting your local club will provide you with access to many knowledgeable individuals who can help you decide what to purchase. It will also provide a great chance to check out the different cars being raced and to ask lots of questions.

Bear in mind that there may be more than one local club and they could all cater for different classes, so you may have to make a number of visits. By observing what goes on at the clubs you should become knowledgeable enough to make a suitable decision regarding what to buy. Not only is racing regularly the quickest way to improve your driving and car set-up skills, but it's also, equally importantly, the path to making a lot of new friends.

BELOW Get out there and have some fun with like-minded people.

LEFT Rally cars offer a combination of some off-road capability with sharp handling.

BELOW Just a few examples of the range of micro scale kits.

BOTTOM LEFT The Xray NT18T in the background is the same size as the Associated RC18T, but the former is nitro-powered and the latter requires batteries.

What scale?

RC cars are sold in a huge range of sizes to suit both the demands of the customer and their intended use. For example, there are micro scale 1:36 and 1:18 kits, with the latter being available in both nitro and electric versions. Obviously the nitro models can't be run indoors, but all of these micro machines are designed for use in smaller areas, as their performance is limited. Putting a 1:24 scale car on a 1:10 circuit will not do it justice.

There are a few kits that fall between the aforementioned micro model scales and the next size up, but the first major sector is 1:12 scale. Most 1:12 kits are either scaled-down touring cars or very impressive carpet racers. The very first were made with a polycarbonate (a plastic material more commonly known as Lexan) chassis and used silicone-coated tyres. Racing took place

Pros and cons

	Electric power	Nitro power
Pros	Quiet	Powerful
	Can be run indoors or outdoors	Can be run for long periods of time
	Easier to comprehend	
Cons	Batteries need recharging	Engine set-up can be awkward
	More than one battery pack is required	Can be more expensive to get set-up initially
		Noisy and smelly

RIGHT One-twelfth scale cars usually race on super-smooth indoor carpet tracks and offer one of the purest forms of RC racing.

BELOW This Kyosho Evolva has a 3.5cc engine and a two-speed gearbox that can propel it to over 70mph.

on polished floors before moving onto tracks laid out on carpet, which resulted in very high grip. These cars can achieve phenomenal speeds and have incredible handling, whilst taking advantage of fairly limited running costs. Although quite simple to look at, they benefit from their light weight and are one of the purest forms of RC racing. However, 1:12 circuit racers are only catered for by specialist clubs so are quite limited, as are the scaled-down touring cars.

If you want something more flexible then 1:10 cars are the best choice as they can be used almost anywhere, from the back garden to the local club.

Going one bigger are 1:8 scale models, which are all nitro-powered and race on purpose-built off- and on-road tracks. These are some of the most impressive models on the market and are very popular at the moment. Kits in this scale currently make up the majority of sales and are becoming the preferred choice of new customers as well as current RC owners looking for a fresh challenge.

There are only a few bigger classes, which can be generalised as 'large scale'. These comprise 1:5 and 1:6 scale cars that require equally large circuits. Both off- and on-road examples are made, and although the latter are driven in competitions recent releases in the off-road market, with their large 22cc two-stroke engines, have become attractive for recreational use.

The combination of scale, on-road or off-road usage, and motive power effectively defines the class of car you'll want to race. Next it's a matter of assessing the different models available within that class to make your final choice. Again the local model shop, your local club and the hobby magazines will prove to be useful allies in making your decision. Check out the features offered on each model and confirm that spare parts are readily available. Don't rush out in a fit of enthusiasm and make a purchase you may end up regretting. Take time deciding what you really want, check to see if the kit is available from your local model shop, and if it isn't try using mail order from another shop. Don't be pushed into buying a particular car just because it happens to be the only one your local specialist has in stock.

RTR versus kit

Many of the current crop of competition kits are supplied as a rolling chassis only, and require other parts in order to get them up and running. For example, electric chassis will require items such as a battery, charger and radio control equipment, so you'll need to add these to your list and be aware that your budget may have to increase to

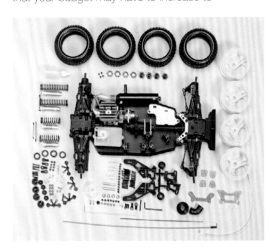

ABOVE Large-scale kits like this Carson can be purchased in both off- and on-road formats to suit the customer's requirements.

LEFT With a kit, you'll gain knowledge of its workings during the build process. *(Ansmann Racing)*

ABOVE Many ready-to-run kits include all the major requirements in the box, so there'll only be minimal further expense.

accommodate them. Likewise, nitro models often don't come with an engine, radio equipment or fuel. In recent years, however, the industry has begun to rectify this by introducing ranges of ready-to-run kits. Alternatively, since for some people much of the enjoyment of the hobby comes from assembling a model from it's component parts, many shops will also offer a bundled price (often

termed a 'deal') that includes not only the basic RC equipment but also the ancillaries that will be required to complete the kit. Nowadays the manufacturers can do this in-house, and RTR kits are supplied to the shop ready-built and checked over, with a decent paint scheme and all the radio installed for you. This offers a number of benefits to all three parties involved, and the biggest winner is the customer.

The RTR boom grew from the concept of providing the customer with a complete package so that their enjoyment could begin immediately. Nitro-powered cars were once plagued by initial setting-up issues and engine unreliability in the hands of inexperienced users, but today's RTR models come with their engines ready-installed, with pre-set carburettors and detailed step-by-step starting instructions, thus ensuring virtually trouble-free starting and running right from the first tank. The radios are set up to the car, the bodyshell is fitted, and any component that needs greasing or threadlocking in place has had it done. RTR kits simply make it easier for the customer – and especially newcomers with limited knowledge – to start enjoying their purchases as soon as they get them home. And the shop also benefits, knowing that the tricky jobs have been done and that there's less chance of the customer coming back with build problems.

An electric car's run-time is dictated by equipment such as the motor and battery. This pack of batteries is 4,200mAh and is the largest capacity currently available.

Run times

Electric RC cars are governed by a number of variables that will determine how long they run between battery recharges. These include the type of motor or motors installed, the capacity of the battery, the gearing, and how you drive it. Rechargeable batteries used to power an electric car will provide run times of approximately 15 minutes, after which – as long as you allow the motor and speed control a few minutes to cool down – you simply replace the empty battery with a fully charged one and the fun can continue. Bear in mind that if you own a fast-charger connected to a

12V car battery, you can fully recharge the battery in approximately 45 minutes.

Unlike the limited capacity of a battery pack, most nitro-powered kits are equipped with easy access fuel tanks that allow refuelling during use. In extreme cases a tank of fuel will only offer around seven or eight minutes' performance if you drive it aggressively, but if you take into consideration fuel stops that take just a few seconds the only restriction is how long the on-board battery lasts. This should be at least an hour, using average-priced cells.

Despite this a large proportion of models are still sold as kits, as this method has its own advantages as well as disadvantages. Firstly, if you build a kit from scratch you get first-hand knowledge of how it goes together, how certain parts work and how you should take sections apart should anything require maintenance or replacement. This knowledge is valuable, as is proven by the fact that some enthusiasts even take RTR kits apart from new to gain a better understanding of them.

You also need to be aware that, for a number of reasons, the price you see on an RTR advertisement or box may still not include everything. Depending upon the specification dictated by the kit manufacturer or distributor, there's a strong chance that the RTR package won't come with fuel, and most nitro kits will require investment in some AA-sized batteries to power the transmitter and the on-board radio equipment. Some will include glow spanners or plug wrenches and fuel bottles or basic glow starters, whilst others won't. This is something that the local dealer can tell you about, so bear it in mind when you're budgeting.

That said, on the whole an RTR kit will save you money over buying the parts individually, although it does mean that you can't purchase it a piece at a time. RTR models tend to use branded components such as engines and radios, so you won't be able to directly compare components and specifications. But if you want to get up and running as quickly as possible, then an RTR model is the way to go. Alternatively, putting the car together can be considered one of the most enjoyable aspects of owning an RC car and the knowledge gained from constructing a chassis will pay dividends in the future.

Whatever you choose, be it a kit or RTR, you should make a list of the required extras, add on a few spare parts too, and ensure that the total amount remains within your budget. With the most important decision made, it's now time to part with that hard-earned cash.

ABOVE How many parts? There are nearly 300 in this Ansmann Virus 1:8 off-road kit. *(Ansmann Racing)*

LEFT This transmitter and fuel bottle come supplied in an RTR package.

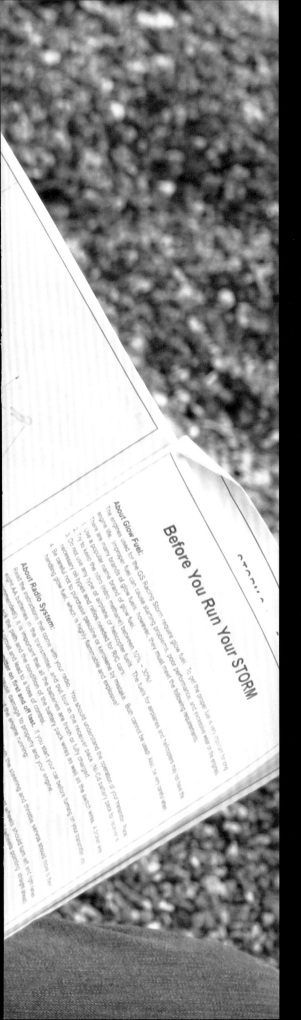

Building an RC car

Follow the instructions	36
Use the correct tools	37
Assembly techniques	40
Building tips	41
Basic set-up	42
Tyre gluing	44
Getting it started	48
Radio gear installation	50
Painting and finishing	58

Follow the instructions

So you've done all the research, decided which car you want and visited the local model shop to make that satisfying purchase. Now comes the most important part: building the car. This can seem very daunting when the box is first opened and all the parts are spread across the table, but by following some simple advice and helpful tips you'll soon have your car up and running. The instructions in the kit, the model shop that sold you the car and the local club are all sources of help should you need advice. The golden rule is to do as much as you can yourself, because that's the fastest way to gain knowledge and experience.

The first thing to do before tackling the actual build is to find the instruction manual and have a good read through it. It will usually provide a list of tools required for assembly and enables you to familiarise yourself with the building process. Most manuals comprise a step-by-step assembly guide that includes written instructions, a list of the parts required for each particular step, and a diagram depicting the parts and where they go.

The quality of model car kits available these days is better than ever. All the parts are designed to fit together properly, and usually without any special machinery or equipment, so the first thing to remember if you're struggling to put something together is not to force it; take it apart and start again. Check the parts – have you got the right ones? And the instructions – are you putting it together correctly? Once you've established you have the right part in the right place, try again. Only very rarely will the parts of a kit be wrong, and if they are, the shop where you bought it will be pleased to put things right.

Use the correct tools

Next, collect the proper tools together. Most kits use Allen screws that require the correct size Allen keys. American kits will require imperial sized keys whilst European and Far Eastern kits will need metric sized versions. Check any other screws to see if you'll need a Phillips or a flat-blade screwdriver. Then check any nuts, again to see whether imperial or metric spanners are required. Don't rely on pliers, clamps, fingers or teeth to hold or tighten the fasteners – always use the correct tools for the job. A small pair of pliers is nevertheless helpful to hold things in place during assembly, and a small vice can be useful for the same purpose. Tweezers can help pick out smaller parts from the bag and hold them during assembly, and you'll need a good modelling knife for cutting fuel hose and removing moulded parts from their sprues.

It's well worth investing in a decent set of tools rather than using the standard Allen keys and spanners that come with most RC car kits. The L-shaped Allen keys can be of poor quality, so that you run the risk of damaging the bolt heads

and potentially hurting yourself. They're also very basic and lack finesse. You may, of course, have already spent a lot of hard-earned cash on the car, so the thought of spending more on specialist tools may be hard to bear, but by choosing carefully and buying quality tools you'll acquire a worthwhile investment that should last you for many years.

Here's a guide to what tools you should buy and why.

Screwdrivers

With a set of small jewellers' screwdrivers, a large flat-blade and a Phillips screwdriver, you should be fully prepared to tackle any type of screw. However tempting it may be, don't use a powered screwdriver. To save weight many screws are made from soft aluminium, and the sudden force from an electric power tool is highly likely to round off the screw head or strip the thread.

When inserting screws into areas that are tricky to access, slip a small piece of fuel tubing over the end of the screwdriver and insert the screw into it. You'll then be able to locate the screw without having to perform a delicate, one-handed balancing act.

Spanners

Small socket spanners are ideal for tightening nuts and are much less likely to damage or scratch them than a pair of pliers. A socket spanner is particularly useful for tightening wheel nuts, and on

OPPOSITE The manual is there to help, so use it! There'll also be set-up tips and other useful information at the back.

LEFT Ditch the standard L-shaped Allen keys that come in a kit and invest in a set of decent tools. Scissors and thin-nose pliers from a DIY store will come in handy.

RIGHT You'll need a soldering iron to install and maintain the motor in an electric-powered kit. Look for one with more than 50W power.

race day may prove to be invaluable if you need to make a last-minute tyre change.

Pliers

A set of conventional pliers and a set of long-nosed ones will be needed. These can be used for a variety of tasks, from twisting and tightening to holding parts steady, for instance when soldering wires together.

Cutters

Three different cutting devices are recommended. A modelling knife equipped with a sharp blade is ideal for cutting out plastic parts and removing any burrs or swarf. A small pair of scissors is likely to be required at some stage, particularly when it's time to install the radio control gear or prepare the bodyshell. And a set of wire cutters will make installing plugs and connectors much easier.

Hex drivers

Although Allen keys are usually provided in the kit for cap head screws, it's far easier to insert these using a solid hex driver. Most model shops carry such tools, many of them packaged by the car manufacturers themselves. With a hex driver far more leverage can be placed on the screw, making it easier to work into tough plastic parts. If the fit is still too tight, drop a small blob of oil onto the end of the screw and it should then screw in first time.

BELOW LEFT A Vernier gauge is a great tool to have, as it has a number of uses. They come in both digital and analogue versions.

BELOW RIGHT Masking tape will be required for spraying the bodyshell.

Vernier gauge

Measuring will be required on some kits, particularly those supplied with adjustable turnbuckles. Using a Vernier gauge to measure the length of these will be much more accurate than guesswork or using a ruler. Standard sliding gauges can be purchased for a reasonable price, but if you can afford a bit more it's possible to get

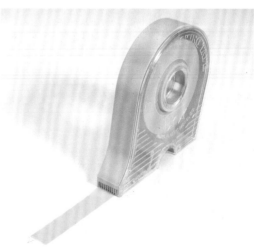

gauges fitted with a digital readout for the ultimate in accuracy.

Soldering iron

If you're building an electric-powered car, a good quality soldering iron is likely to be required. The wires from the speed control have to be soldered to small metal lugs on the motor, and it may be necessary to install connectors to plug into the on-board battery pack. You may also need to build the battery packs themselves when you purchase top-of-the-range matched racing packs that are often supplied as individual cells. For this you need to make sure the soldering iron has a power rating of at least 50W and has a large tip fitted that will hold the heat required to solder cells together. Good quality soldering irons are available that will connect to either the mains or a 12V power supply. More expensive gas-powered types are also available.

Tape

The following types of tape are typically used for model cars: insulating tape for securing and protecting wiring; double-sided tape for attaching components to the chassis; fibreglass reinforced tape for securing heavy items that may move;

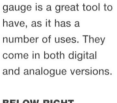

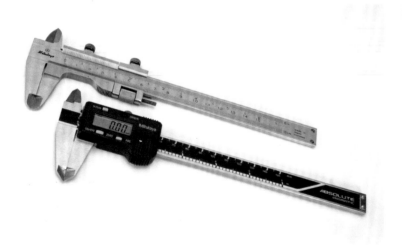

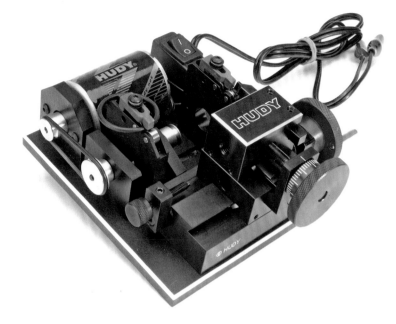

masking tape for marking out paint schemes on the bodyshell; and gaffer or duct tape for repairing the bodyshell and protecting the underside of the chassis. Most of these are available from model shops, car accessory stockists and DIY stores.

Brushes

Keeping a car clean not only improves its appearance, but also helps to prevent wear and tear. A selection of different-sized brushes is ideal for removing surface dust. Use them when building the kit to remove small residue created by filing or cutting, and dust the car down after each race to keep it in tip-top condition.

Special tools and helpers

As well as the standard types of tool already mentioned, there are lots of special tools and helpers available to the RC car builder. These are designed to make certain tasks easier and most are available from model shops. They include such things as glow plug spanners, turnbuckle wrenches, ball cup drivers and reamers. All of these are designed to do specific jobs and will help you to build and maintain your car more easily.

Other items that are useful to have include a car stand, motor stand, shock absorber holder and battery pack assembly jig. However, these aren't essential when you first take up model car driving and they can be bought later on, when you'll find that they make life a bit easier.

Motor lathe

The motor lathe is a specialist piece of equipment designed to enable you to refinish the copper on a motor's commutator. This improves the electrical contact made with the motor brushes and dramatically improves performance. They were once seen as exotic items only used by top competition-level drivers, but have now become a common sight at most race meetings. They work just like a full-size lathe and usually have a

diamond cutting-tool that skims the top layer of copper from the motor's commutator, which may have been burnt and grooved by the brushes, leaving it fresh and true. As more drivers move over to brushless motors the need to carry a motor lathe will diminish, as these motors don't require the same amount of maintenance.

Powered multi-tools

If you're thinking of using electric-powered tools a cordless screwdriver isn't recommended, as depending upon the application and material used you'll require different torque and speed settings, and the human hand is much more sensitive and flexible. However, there are circumstances where a powered device is invaluable, for example when trimming a body, drilling a hole or grinding a part. At such times it's useful to have one of the range of powered multi-tools that are available today, such as those from Dremel. They include both

TOP LEFT You can use a paintbrush or toothbrush to help clean your chassis, but companies like Upgrade RC offer a range of specialist brushes.

ABOVE A lathe is used to remove the damaged copper off the surface of a brushed motor's commutator.

BELOW Sold in both hobby and DIY stores, a powered rotary tool like this Dremel is worth having in your toolbox.

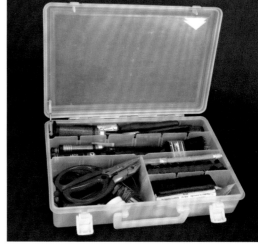

ABOVE LEFT A large toolbox will be useful to store your RC equipment as well as some spares and accessories...

ABOVE RIGHT ...but you don't need a large toolbox to carry the most important items.

BELOW Threadlock is a cheap item but a must-have if you want to prevent your RC vehicle from breaking down.

mains and battery-powered rotary tools with a selection of cutting wheels, drum sanders and brushes. With adjustable speed settings, keyless operation and often a range of attachments, such tools are perfect for RC modellers.

Toolbox

It helps to have somewhere to store your collection of tools. Though to start off with you can keep them in the box the kit originally came in, it's best to invest in a dedicated toolbox. Specialist toolboxes can be purchased from most model shops, but it's also worth taking a look in your local DIY store. If you're feeling really ambitious you can even build one yourself. It's worth going for a reasonably large toolbox from day one, since it doesn't usually take too long to fill it. Once you've got the racing bug you'll soon be buying tyres, spares, bodyshells and

all sorts of things that promise to make your car go faster for longer, and you'll need somewhere to put them – in fact you'll find you accumulate spares far more quickly than you throw them away. Most racers have an inbuilt belief that the tool or spare part they need may be the very one they inadvertently left at home, so to avoid this happening they always take everything with them.

Assembly techniques

Vibration can be a problem on a model car, whether it's caused by the engine operating non-stop at different frequencies on a nitro model, or simply as a result of general running on an electric car, so the build is all about ensuring that things don't come undone. Threadlock is therefore a very useful item to have around, and may even be provided in the kit – just make sure you use threadlock where the screws need to be undone when required, and not studlock, which will result in them never coming out again!

Certain parts are designed to be run-in, so as you use the car they'll loosen up. During assembly it may seem that some parts are a bit tight. If this is in the transmission, make sure that the tightness isn't something rubbing or binding against something else. Everything should move freely and evenly and have the same 'feel' as it's moved, not notchy or sticky. Having a free transmission will help the car to run smoothly, quietly and more efficiently.

When assembling shafts, try each bearing separately as you build. When tightening bearing caps, or nuts on the end of shafts, check the rotation of the shaft as it's tightened up to make

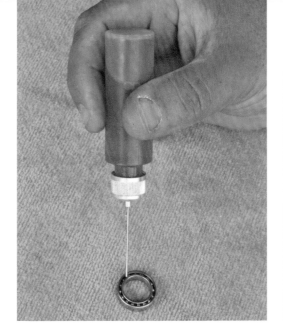

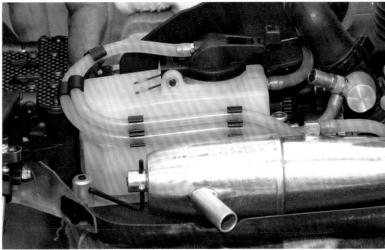

ABOVE LEFT Metal bearings like this one require regular oiling for lubrication.

ABOVE The fuel pipe on a nitro kit must be kept in good condition and held out of the way of rotating parts by means of clips or something similar.

sure it rotates properly even when the nut is tight – unless, of course, the nut is supposed to hold that particular shaft stationary.

Suspension movement must be free, and without play. Don't use drills or reamers to make holes bigger during assembly. Once each corner of the car is assembled, but before the wheels, roll bars, and springs and dampers go on, raise the suspension and let it fall. It should drop under it's own weight. If it doesn't, but will fall with a light tap, leave it alone. But if the assembly is stiff take the parts off one by one and test it again after removing each. When the 'offender' has been found, check the best way to make movement freer and then reassemble. This can be time consuming, but will pay you back in spades with better handling and longer component life. Use the same method to make sure the steering assembly is free but not sloppy.

Engines must be bolted in tightly and you can use a little threadlock on all the nuts and bolts; the same goes for any exhaust supports, transmission parts and belt tensioners. Although these will be checked after the first couple of races, now is the time to make sure they're correctly tightened and won't come undone during the car's first run.

The bodyshell may require painting. Use paints designed for the Lexan polycarbonate material from which bodies are now largely made, and paint-specific masking tape to mask out the car's windows if none are provided in the kit. Although fancy paint jobs look great, they can be difficult and time consuming to accomplish and it's still possible to achieve a good looking professional finish using a single colour and the proper placement of stickers (also known as decals).

Check the position of the body posts and drill holes for them before painting the bodyshell, as it's easier to see and get it right at this stage. For a nitro car, after the body's painted cut a hole in the front and rear windows to allow air to circulate around the engine – this is essential and is mentioned in most kit instructions. Some nitro kits may also require a hole in the side of the body to allow the exhaust pipe to exit.

Fit the body to the chassis and check that the wheels don't touch the wheel arches when the suspension moves up and down, or with the steering on full lock either left or right. Trim if necessary.

On a nitro car, check the run of the fuel pipe to make sure it won't get snagged on any of the moving linkages for suspension, throttle, steering or braking. Where possible hold it in place using small tie-wraps linked to parts of the chassis; it's a good idea to allow the pipe to move a bit.

Before fitting the air filter, put some special air filter oil on it in accordance with the instructions, either those with the car or those on the bottle. This is essential to ensure that dust and dirt don't get into the engine and wear it out prematurely. Make sure that filter oil is in the kit, or get it included in your deal.

Building tips

Most modern RC cars are finished very well and don't require as much DIY work during building as they did a few years ago. But there are still important things to take care of when building.

Check that the suspension arms, castor blocks, steering blocks and hubs all move freely around the hinge pins. If any of these are at all stiff or binding they'll need loosening off; just be careful not to create any slop. A good tip is to take a spare hinge pin and roughen the surface with some sandpaper. Then use this rather than

RIGHT The drop test – make sure that the suspension moves freely by taking the shock off.

BELOW The wishbone should fall under its own weight. If it doesn't, you'll need to find out why and correct the problem.

FAR RIGHT Modern day set-up systems, such as this one from Hudy, allow you to check all your settings.

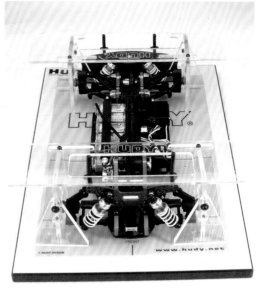

use a drill or reamer to clean the holes in the parts and you'll get a perfect, free-moving, slop-free suspension arm.

Chassis flex can dramatically change the way a car handles. Generally the more flex, the more steering, so experiment with different top decks. Sometimes removing a little material from a top deck to allow the chassis to flex more will give you more steering. It's a good idea to try this out using a spare top deck.

As far as hop-up parts are concerned, most kits come with many of these upgraded parts as standard these days, but good bearings and carbide differential balls are two items that are worth investing in, as they can improve the performance of your car.

Basic set-up

Below are the things that you should pay particular attention to if you want to set up a balanced car that's easy to drive and handles well.

Chassis balance – Good balance in the chassis is very important. What you're basically looking for is a car that leans evenly front-to-rear. If the car dives at the front it'll become hard to drive, and the same is true if it 'dumps' the rear leaving a corner.

Achieving this is very different from chassis to chassis. Cell layout, radio layout, motor position, shock pick-up points – all vary slightly with each manufacturer, so though you may look at various cars and think they look the same if you look more closely you'll see they're actually very different.

Weight distribution – Aim to set this up 50:50 front-to-rear and side-to-side.

Suspension – You may find you need harder shock oil front-to-rear or vice versa, and it's the same with springs. Sometimes you may want the same front and back. To check it, place the car race-ready but without its body on a flat surface

LEFT Using a gauge to measure ride height. This should be checked front and rear.

BELOW Droop tools are an accurate way to make sure that the settings are the same left and right.

and feel the stiffness front-to-rear. The rear should feel slightly harder than the front. This is a good starting point. The only way to really find out if the suspension is set up correctly is to try to run the car.

Ride height – This needs to be set as low as you can get away with in order to lower the centre of gravity and improve the car's handling characteristics. With an on-road touring car

start with 6mm rear and 5.5mm front outdoors, and come down by 1mm all round when running indoors.

Droop – This is the amount of downward movement the wishbones have when connected to the suspension. It should be set 1mm less front-to-rear – about 4mm on a droop gauge rear and 5mm on the front work as a starting point for most 1:10 scale on-road cars.

RIGHT The diffs can suffer from dirt getting in and ruining their performance.

Differentials – These need to be maintained regularly. A stiff or gritty diff can destroy the handling of your car. Also a common mistake by racers is to leave the diff too loose. Make sure it doesn't slip under power.

Bodyshell – This makes a huge difference to the handling of an RC car. Look at what the fast drivers are using and test as many as you can to find the one that suits your driving style best. Always pay attention to the way you mount it. Make sure it sits square to the chassis, that the arches are in the right places, and make sure the wing is mounted as high as legally allowed.

BELOW Check the bodyshell regularly for rips and dents, as these can all affect the handling.

By following these simple set-up rules you should have a good basic starting point for most makes of car. You'll then be able to make small adjustments to all these areas to fine tune the car for where you intend to run it. Just remember to make a note of each thing you change so that you can tell what difference each adjustment makes and can always revert back to the standard set-up if you lose your way.

Tyre gluing

The most important components on any RC car are the tyres. They're not only what keeps the car in contact with the ground, they're also an essential ingredient for fine tuning its handling. Keeping them stuck to the track is one thing, but keeping them stuck to the wheels is quite another.

With the amount of power available and the high cornering speeds of today's RC cars the tyres are under an immense amount of pressure, with the forces involved constantly trying to pull them off the rims. Making sure they're glued firmly on is therefore vital, so here's a step-by-step guide to successful tyre building.

Drill the wheels – Two small holes should first be drilled at the top and bottom of each wheel using a small drill or reamer. As the tyres are semi-pneumatic the holes allow them to enlarge

LEFT Poor tyre gluing can ruin a race. This picture was taken at a recent World Championship.

BELOW Using a reamer, make two 4mm diameter holes in the rim.

and deflate during use as air is pushed in and out of the tyre and insert. This helps the tyre to make good contact with the track surface and so increases traction.

Clean the rims and tyres – The plastic wheel rims and rubber tyres are both coated with a chemical releasing agent. This is deposited during the manufacturing process and must be removed if the glue is to achieve a strong bond. Use solvent such as motor spray or lighter fluid on a tissue or rag to clean this residue from the rims and tyre beads. It may be worth testing a small area first to make sure the solvent you're using doesn't react with either the plastic or rubber.

FAR LEFT It's worth wiping the gluing surface of the rim before you mount the tyre.

LEFT Motor cleaner is perfect for removing the mould release agent from a tyre.

RIGHT Place the insert inside the tyre and make sure it's seated correctly.

BELOW Carefully pull the tyre and insert over the rim and work it into position before gluing.

BELOW RIGHT Using dedicated tyre glue, lift the bead of the tyre and place a small amount of glue in the gap.

Add insert – Some tyres are supplied with an insert, but if they're not you'll have to choose which one to use. Just like tyres, these are available in a range of different compounds. A soft insert will make the assembled tyre feel softer and should increase available grip, but it may also make the tyre wear faster. Alternatively, a harder insert will stop the tyre from deforming quite so

much, therefore reducing both grip and wear rate. Once you're happy with your chosen insert fit it into the tyre and make sure it's seated properly all the way round.

Fit the tyre – Now take the tyre and insert and carefully stretch them over the wheel. Try to do this as smoothly as possible to avoid twisting or unseating the insert. Once the tyre is completely on the wheel, go all the way around the rim and make sure the bead of the tyre is pushed into the moulded grooves on the edge of the wheel. Once you're happy with the fit, go round the whole assembly and check that everything seems seated correctly and that the tyre is round, with no flat spots or high points. If it isn't seated properly, carefully pick up the tread and work it until the profile becomes consistent. You can roll the tyre between your hands to help the seating process.

Glue on – The tyre is now ready for gluing. Always use a good quality cyanoacrylate adhesive, which is better known as superglue. Lighter weight superglue is easier to run around the edges and will also dry much faster than a thicker variety, but care must be taken not to use too much or to let the glue run over onto the tyre surface. To start with lift up a small portion of the tyre bead on one side and drop in a small amount of superglue. Then push the bead firmly back into place and allow it to dry for a few seconds before repeating the process all the way round the tyre. Remember that when it comes to using superglue, less is definitely more. If you do accidentally get glue on the tyre tread, don't panic. Let it dry and then use

sandpaper or a Dremel fitted with a small sanding drum to remove it.

Check edges – Once you've glued the tyre all the way round leave it to dry while you tackle the next one. Then go back to the first one and glue up the other side, and so on until both sides of all four tyres have been glued. As the light superglue dries quite quickly you should then be able to go back to the first tyre to inspect your handiwork. Check that the tyre is properly seated and secure all the way round. If it isn't, manipulate the bead by pushing and pulling the edge of the tyre to ensure that it's seated flat and tight to the rim without any gaps. For added security you can now very carefully put a small drop of superglue on the tyre sidewall where it meets the rim and let it run all the way round to seal the edge.

Leave to dry – Now leave all the tyres in a warm dry place to allow the glue to cure properly. If you're gluing tyres between races at the track you should be able to use them straight away, but if possible try and build your tyres the night before you really need them, as this will allow the glue plenty of time to set and lessen the chance of a tyre coming off in a race.

Mark the wheels – So that you can remember what tyre compound and insert combination is mounted, write it on the wheel using a fine permanent marker pen. One tip from some of the top drivers is that if you don't want others to know what tyres you're running you should write this information inside the wheel hex in the centre. You'll have to write very small, but once

the wheels are fitted on the car no one will know what tyres you're using.

Use or store – If you've built the new tyres up at the track, you may be intending to use them straight away. If you've glued them at home and won't be using them for a while the best way to store them is in a sealed plastic bag. Resealable

LEFT Make the glue run around the edge as an extra measure.

BELOW Leave the glued tyres out of the way so that the glue can fully cure.

BELOW You may have a number of different tyres and compounds so make a note of it on the inside of the rim.

Health and safety

When using superglue, particularly the very runny lightweight variety, always handle it with great care. Use the glue sparingly, wear some eye protection, and avoid getting glue on your fingers or clothing. It's also a good idea to carry a bottle of superglue release agent in your toolbox in case of emergencies.

Pre-glued tyres

If building your own tyres seems like hard work, it's now possible to buy most popular compounds of tyre pre-glued on wheels. These are bonded firmly to the rims using special gluing processes that are extremely strong and reliable. Using such tyres saves a lot of time and effort, and when you take the separate costs of wheels, inserts, tyres and glue into consideration they're also very good value for money.

RIGHT If you're not going to use the tyres straight away place them in a resealable plastic bag.

freezer bags available from the supermarket are ideal and will stop the rubber drying out. Your brand new tyres are now ready for use.

Getting it started

Something that builders of electric cars don't have to deal with is getting the engine started for the first time. This can be quite stressful as there's always the worry that it won't start, but the trick is

to follow the instructions to the letter, because experience shows that they usually will.

All nitro cars will need a glow plug heater/starter, a small device that connects to the glow plug and provides the means of starting the engine. Cut a hole in the body so that the glow starter can be used with the bodyshell in place.

Some cars have a pull starter. Make sure that you can access this with the bodyshell on, as otherwise it will be frustrating having to remove the clips and shell each time. Cutting a hole in a side

RIGHT Starting a nitro engine is easy if you follow the instruction manual but experience is always beneficial.

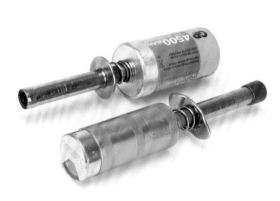

window of the body may help, by making sure that it's easy to get to in a hurry even with cold hands! Although cars are usually started with the body off, a stall just before the start of your race causes less panic if you can get the glow starter on and pull the cord without removing the body.

Other cars may need a starter box. Try and sort this out when buying the kit, since many shops will do a deal if it's bought at the same time. You may need to adjust the positioning devices on the starter box so that the starter wheel is correctly positioned under the flywheel. If you have a starting device that uses a cordless drill a hole must be made in the body to allow access.

Once the engine has been started for the first time, follow the running-in (or breaking-in) instructions. However tempting it may be, don't use full throttle until the stated amount of time has been spent running the car. After every run, stop the car and check all your assembly work, looking for anything that might have come loose during running.

Special attention should be paid to engine mountings, transmission parts, wheels, tyres and suspension parts. Any faults found must be traced back to source before the car is run again, so take this opportunity to learn about the car, and things that can be adjusted or need to be checked. After two or three runs, especially if they're on a deserted tarmac or concrete area

ABOVE LEFT Glow starters come in a range of designs but they all do the same job.

ABOVE An engine with a pull-start arrangement.

LEFT As the performance of engines increases there's a greater likelihood that you'll require a starter box.

ABOVE Correct set up of radio gear such as the servo will ensure that you achieve maximum performance.

where there'll be more dust, take the air filter off and wash it out in hot, soapy water. Re-oil the air filter as before and refit it.

Once the running-in process is complete, make a thorough check of the car before racing it. Remove the engine mounting bolts (one at a time to avoid changing the gear mesh) to make sure that the threadlock is in place, and refit with another small drop of threadlock. This will confirm that your assembly procedure is correct and avoid problems later.

Radio gear installation

Correct installation and setting up of the radio control equipment – often referred to as the 'radio gear' – in your car is critical. It's what connects you, the driver, to the car and decides what the car's actually going to do, so it's worth taking time to fit everything in neatly and check it's all set up and working properly on the bench before attempting to run the car.

Correctly setting up of the radio gear in any model car is important, but probably more so with a nitro car than an electric, for a number of reasons. Firstly, a nitro uses two servos, one for the steering and one to control the throttle, rather than a servo and electronic speed control.

Secondly, the throttle servo in particular has to be set up carefully and accurately if it's to work properly. And thirdly, unlike the majority of electric models a nitro-powered car requires a dedicated onboard battery to power the receiver and servos.

This is another area of a nitro kit where you need to spend some time preparing your car and radio on the bench before running it. Even then, only by running your car will you be able to fine-tune the throttle, brake settings, steering travel and trim.

Choose your radio carefully as it's important to be able to adjust the servo throw end-point (how far the servo travels in each direction) for proper set-up and operation. Radio sets designed for use with nitro-powered models also often have a throttle mix setting which allows fine adjustment of the throttle and brake. These radios are referred to as three-channel sets.

Fine-tuning

Getting the transmitter correctly tuned for your nitro car is crucial if the engine is to run properly and you want to avoid frustrating engine cuts. Although much of the initial tuning can be adjusted by the high- and low-speed needle valves, fine-tuning is often made using the trims on the transmitter.

Correct braking set-up is also vital on a nitro car since, unlike an electric motor, a nitro engine doesn't provide any natural braking effect at neutral. Instead, all the braking has to be input by the driver through the transmitter. The amount and force of braking is also fine-tuned using the transmitter trims.

Making the link

Placement of the radio gear in a nitro car is usually dictated by the radio plate supplied with the kit. One servo is used for the steering and a second is used to control the throttle. In an electric car placement of the steering servo is usually determined by the chassis design, while the rest of the equipment, the receiver and speed control, can be fitted in wherever there's room and they look neatest.

It's best to follow your individual car's instruction manual when fitting and setting up the radio gear, as every model is different. While the steering is usually quite a simple set-up with track rods connected to a servo saver, the throttle linkage can be a little more complicated and requires careful setting up and patient fine-tuning if it's to work correctly.

A twin-arm servo horn is usually used for the throttle. These are often supplied with the kit, or you may find that one is supplied with your radio gear. The throttle linkage is connected to one side of the servo horn while the brake linkage is connected to the other. As the servo turns it will either pull or push the throttle linkage, to open or close the carburettor to allow more or less fuel into the engine and therefore increase or decrease engine speed. At the same time it will pull or push the brake linkage to either engage the clutch and release the brakes or disengage the clutch and increase braking. When the servo is in the neutral position the engine should be at idle with the brakes released and the clutch disengaged. Getting this action right is the key to making the car idle, accelerate and brake smoothly and efficiently.

Throttle servo

When connecting the throttle, the first thing to do before attaching the servo horn is to centre the servo. This is done by making sure that the trim is in the centre and, with a computer radio, by making sure the sub-trim is set to zero. Next check the servo is going in the right direction. You may have to change the direction of the servo by using the servo reverse switch on the transmitter.

Once you're happy the servo is centred and going in the correct direction you can attach the servo horn. The linkages are then attached to the horn, adjusting their length as necessary and in accordance with your model's instructions. There's

TOP With a nitro-powered model, the servos, receiver and receiver battery all fit in allocated places.

ABOVE A close-up shot of the all-important throttle and brake linkage. Incorrect set-up here can potentially cause problems.

LEFT The throttle servo on a nitro-powered kit requires a servo horn with a connecting point at each end.

usually a spring located on each side of where the linkage is attached to the servo horn, which is designed to take up any play and protect the servo from overloading as a result of extra travel.

Speed controls (ESCs)

Electronic speed controls or speedos, as they're commonly known, are used in electric RC cars to control the motor. They replace the throttle servo, taking the signal directly from the receiver and transforming it into a current drawn from the battery supply that feeds the motor. In addition to all of this the speed control provides a suitable supply voltage for the receiver and steering servo and, in some cases, even a cooling fan for the motor.

Modern speed controls are very easy to set up. Many come with a single-touch button set-up with an LED light indicator, whilst some use clever software programming that automatically tunes itself to the transmitter each time it's switched on!

Tip

It's a good idea to replace the spring on the braking side of the throttle linkage with some silicone fuel tubing, as this allows for a more progressive action to the braking.

However, the ease of set up belies an impressive array of tuneable functions, especially on higher performing speed controls that enable them to alter the way current is fed into the motor. Basically, once the signal has been interpreted from the receiver, the speed control is a highly efficient switch. By altering the frequency that the switch opens and closes (the drive frequency), the speed control can actually help to keep the motor running cooler and provide more 'feel' to the driver. Regenerative braking is also a common feature, which effectively uses the dynamo principle of induction to provide good use of the back EMF generated when braking.

Large 'power' capacitors have become commonplace on many speed controls as they provide a power reserve that helps provide more instant power on throttle applications where otherwise, even with today's high power batteries, sudden demands from the motor can cause the supply voltage to drop. This makes the car 'lag' during acceleration and can even cause the receiver voltage to go below critical supply level.

Testing time

The best way to check your radio set-up is with the car on the bench, its chassis supported so that the wheels are well clear of the surface. Switch on your transmitter, then the radio in the car, and start the engine. If everything's adjusted correctly the engine should sit and idle when the transmitter trim is central. If the wheels creep slightly you can make fine adjustments by adjusting the transmitter trim back slightly. If the

car keeps stalling you can increase the idle speed by pushing the trim forwards.

Other things to check are that when the car is at full throttle, with the carburettor fully open, there isn't excess servo travel and strain on the linkage and servo horn. If there is, you may have to adjust the servo travel end-point. The same applies to the brakes, as you don't want to put undue strain on the servo or linkages during operation in case they should fail when you're running the car.

When all the radio gear is adjusted properly, your nitro car should idle without the engine cutting, accelerate smoothly and consistently, and brake progressively without locking the wheels.

The important thing is to take your time and make sure everything is right before running the car, then you'll be all set for a lot of fast fun.

Similar principles apply for electric-powered models. Centring the steering servo so that there are equal levels of travel in both directions is essential for the consistent operation of any model and is achieved by simply turning on the transmitter and receiver whilst ensuring that all of the transmitter trims are in the neutral position.

The same applies for any electric car that utilises a servo for the throttle application. The procedure for setting up an Electronic Speed Controller (ESC) is somewhat different, and will

ABOVE LEFT You have independent front- and rear-wheel braking on a nitro-powered off-road chassis.

ABOVE You can check the braking level between the front and rear by operating the servo manually.

LEFT The braking level on the front or rear can be altered on the knurled nuts. Undoing the nut will increase the braking effect and vice versa.

Receiver packs

A dedicated onboard battery pack is used to power the radio equipment in a nitro car and some electric cars. Most ready-to-run cars are supplied with a battery cradle in which to fit standard AA dry cells. More advanced cars usually use a rechargeable battery pack designed for the job.

There are a number of advantages to using a 'proper' rechargeable receiver pack over normal AA cells. The first and possibly most important is their size. Tiny receiver cells can be made up into packs in much the same way as the larger sub-C size cells used to power an electric car. They can be soldered together in a variety of different configurations to suit any particular application. Space in modern RC cars is often tight and these small cells will fit in a lot more easily. Being smaller also means they're lighter, saving valuable weight in a racing-oriented car.

These days, if you don't want to have to make up your own it's quite easy to buy ready-made receiver packs that are shrink-wrapped with a plug fitted.

Being rechargeable means receiver packs can be used many times and easily topped up before each race. Receiver pack cells are available as both NiMH and NiCd, and like their larger sub-C counterparts they have to be treated carefully and charged correctly.

Many of the latest chargers have special settings dedicated to recharging lower capacity packs. If you intend to charge receiver packs with a normal charger you have to make sure the current is turned right down to between 0.5 and 1 amp. Charging at a higher rate may cause the cells to overheat and in some circumstances explode!

Just like racing packs used in an electric car, receiver packs should be discharged and stored properly when not in use. Most dischargers will deal with receiver packs, but a number of special discharging and cycling products are now coming onto the market including dedicated discharge boards.

differ depending on the make of the ESC you're using. The common principle, though, is that once the ESC is put into set-up mode (normally achieved by holding down the set up button whilst powering-on), the throttle neutral point, full throttle high point and full reverse points are all programmed and stored into the ESC by holding the transmitter at the various throttle input points and pressing the set up button. Although each ESC will be slightly different, most use a series of coloured LED lights to help denote the program setting that's being stored. On high-end ESCs the number and sequence of these LEDs can also be used as a diagnostic tool to check different settings, such as brake power and initial punch (ie how aggressive the throttle response is).

Neat wiring

Neat installation of the radio control equipment in a model car not only makes it look better, but can also help improve performance and lessen the chances of a breakdown. Here are some tips for achieving a better installation:

Coil your receiver leads – This is achieved by wrapping your receiver lead around a thin-shafted tool such as a screwdriver or Allen key. Wrap it nice and tight and hold it there for a few seconds. Then slide the tool out and plug the lead into the receiver. You can stretch the coiled lead to its necessary length whilst maintaining the cool coiled look.

ABOVE Neat wiring takes time and a few small pieces of equipment to achieve the best results.

LEFT Use a screwdriver to coil your receiver leads.

RIGHT Fit a protective cap over the end of the aerial tube.

Don't leave aerial wire floating – A loose wire hanging out of the top of your aerial tube is asking for trouble. To prevent it you can either make a neat coil of the wire at the base of the tube or run the extra wire down the outside. Use a rubber aerial tip to keep things neat at the top, and secure the extra either with a small rubber O-ring or some electrical tape.

Cut wires down to the correct length – Wires that are too long or too short aren't ideal. Make sure that when you're wiring up a car you make the wires the right length. They shouldn't be tight or flop around, but bear in mind that if you have alternative battery positions you may need to allow a little extra length to reach the terminals.

Fix down switches – Use either a cable tie through a hole in the chassis, or some good quality double-sided tape. If a switch isn't in a fixed position it can be a lot of grief for your mechanic to find it, and if it falls outside the body it can easily be ripped off.

Tie or shrink wires – Either use cable ties to neaten wires and keep them out of the way or use some heatshrink to hold two wires together.

BELOW Short wires reduce the risk of damage and ensure maximum performance.

RIGHT Too many racers leave switches floating. Just use some double-sided tape to hold them down.

FAR RIGHT Cable ties can help to keep the wires where you want them.

FAR LEFT Two layers of double-sided tape can help to absorb shocks through the chassis.

FAR LEFT If you can fit your servo in place with posts, it's best to use them. One is better than none.

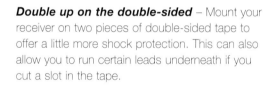

LEFT Prevent your aerial tube from coming out by securing it with a grub screw.

Double up on the double-sided – Mount your receiver on two pieces of double-sided tape to offer a little more shock protection. This can also allow you to run certain leads underneath if you cut a slot in the tape.

Secure your servo – Fit the steering servo to your car using servo posts if possible rather than sticking it to the chassis with servo tape. This will give it a firmer anchor and make sure all the servo's power goes into the car's steering, which will sharpen up its handling.

Fix the aerial – Use a grub screw on your aerial mount to hold the aerial tube in place and prevent it from being pulled out in a crash.

Solder wires on – Soldering wires to your motor not only offers the best possible electrical connection with the least amount of power loss, but it also makes the whole installation a lot neater. Just be careful not to use too much solder or hold the iron on the joint for too long.

ABOVE Dispense with bullet-type connectors and solder the wires directly to your motor.

Keep it low – Try to mount as much of your radio gear as low down on the chassis as possible. This keeps the centre of gravity low and helps to balance the handling of the car.

LEFT Mount all your radio equipment as low as possible for better handling.

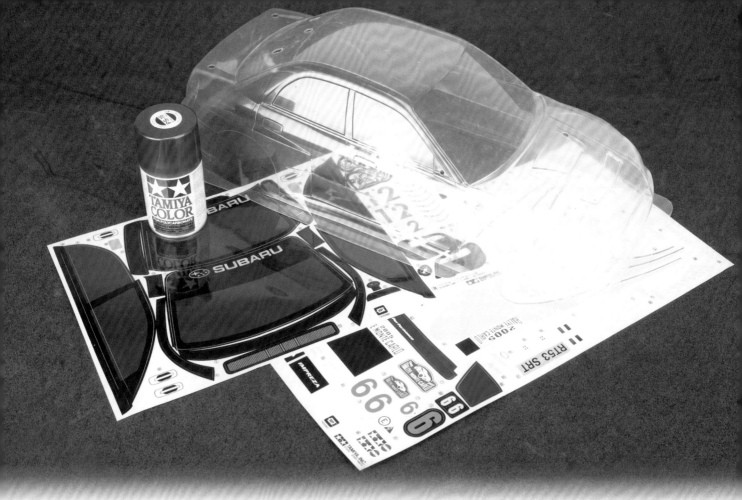

ABOVE Even a one-colour paint scheme and a few decals can make a car look like its been finished to the highest standard.

Painting and finishing

One of the most satisfying parts of building a new model car is painting the bodyshell. It means the car's nearly finished, and topping it off with a smart body with a great paint job really makes it look the part and turns a functional rolling chassis into a sleek racing machine.

Spraying bodies is a true art form, with some racers getting as much enjoyment out of their painting as they do from their racing. It goes without saying that the end result is usually directly proportional to the amount of effort you

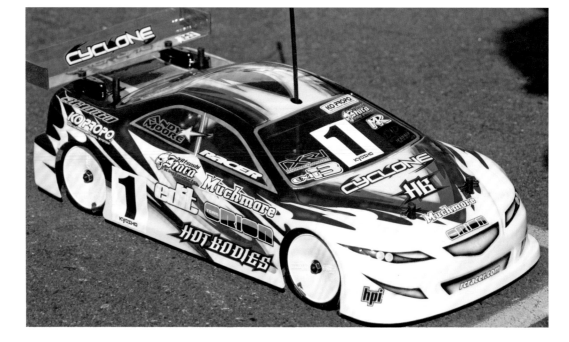

RIGHT Racers paint their bodyshells in unique schemes. By adopting a set design, their cars become instantly recognisable on the track by other drivers and spectators alike.

put in. Take time to draw the colour scheme first, carefully apply the required layers of masking tape, paint from dark to light, leave to dry between coats, and you can end up with a real masterpiece. Pull the bodyshell out of the packet and immediately aerosol a single coat of paint onto it and the results tend to be slightly less impressive! Thankfully even simple paint schemes can be made to look good with the right stickers, so even if you're not a budding artist you can still come up with an acceptable creation.

Which bodyshell you choose may be determined by a number of factors. You may have just built your first car and it came with a body, or you might fancy a change and have bought a replacement shell, or you could be looking to improve your car's performance and handling characteristics by fitting it with the latest body with the best aerodynamics. Whatever the reason, one thing is certain: you want it to look fantastic and for everyone to notice it, and the only way that's going to happen is if you put in a little hard work preparing and painting it. A well finished and mounted bodyshell not only makes your car look better, but is also a very satisfying achievement.

Just like building the kit, there are a few simple rules that need to be followed in order to produce a winning design. The first thing you have to understand when it comes to painting a Lexan polycarbonate bodyshell is that they're painted on the *inside*. This may seem odd at first, but all becomes 'clear' in the end. The reason is fairly simple: painting the shell on the inside means you get a nice smooth finish on the outside that's not going to get scratched and ruined too easily. The design can be further enhanced by the application of stickers or decals to the outside.

Tools required

Before you can start preparing and painting your bodyshell you'll have to get a few tools together. These include curved scissors for cutting out the wheelarches and a file or sandpaper for smoothing off any rough edges. A powered multi-tool such as a Dremel is also sometimes useful for smoothing off and drilling holes, but it must be used carefully, as it can do a lot of damage in the wrong hands. If it's your first bodyshell, it may be better to stick to hand tools. A pair of straight scissors and a modelling knife or scalpel are also useful items for cutting out the bodyshell.

The inside of a bodyshell usually has a pretty smooth finish which needs to be scratched, or keyed, slightly to help the paint to adhere. This can be achieved by using a scouring pad when you wash the body to remove greasy deposits (see below). The resultant tiny surface scratches won't show up when the shell is painted.

Some bodies are supplied with window masks. These are stuck on the inside of the windows and make life a lot easier. If your kit or body doesn't come with masking, you'll need some masking tape. This can also be used to isolate any areas you intend to paint a different colour. Finally, you will of course need some paint. This can be purchased from model shops and comes either in aerosol spray-cans or in small pots that can be used with an airbrush.

Whichever method of paint application you choose it should be possible to create an effective colour scheme in a relatively short amount of time by following some simple steps.

Preparing the body

While the bodyshell is still a lump of clear plastic it's a good idea to cut and drill the holes for the body posts and aerial – it's much easier to accurately align holes when you can still see through the shell. Start by placing the uncut shell over the car and accurately mark the position of the body posts and aerial. Take care to ensure these are in the correct position, as it's all too easy to end up with a body that's mounted either too far forwards or backwards or is even lopsided. If you already have a used body of the same style, a good tip is to slip this

BELOW A selection of tools that you'll require to spray and fit a bodyshell.

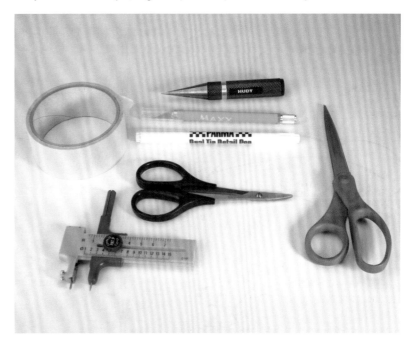

with a modelling knife and then gently bend the plastic over to break it apart. Either method will work, but the aim is to end up with a clean cut.

Now it's time to cut out the wheelarches. Most bodyshells will have trim lines for the front wheelarches moulded into them, but the rears are usually left blank to allow for varying wheelbases. Using one of the pieces cut out for the front wheelarches as a template is a good way to ensure the remaining arches are marked and cut to a similar shape. Use a sharp pair of curved scissors to cut out the arches and then smooth off the edges with fine sandpaper or a large 'half-moon' file.

Once you've cut out the bodyshell it needs to be thoroughly washed in warm soapy water to remove any grease. As mentioned earlier, it's a good idea to use a scouring pad so as to lightly scuff the inside of the shell so that paint can adhere to it more easily. Rinse it off with clean water and dry it thoroughly with a lint-free cloth or towel, making sure you remove any water that might have got into the nooks and crannies of the moulding.

Masking out

Your next job is to mask out the paint scheme. As mentioned earlier, many of the latest bodyshells are supplied with suitable window masks, which speeds up the masking process and helps to make sure that the windows are a better shape. If the car is to be a single colour, this will probably be the only masking required, but if a more complex design is to be attempted some quality masking tape will need to be applied to mark out the paint scheme.

Always be sure to use good quality masking

over the top of the new shell and mark where the mounting holes were.

Use a drill or reamer to carefully cut out the holes, smoothing them off with a round file. The clear unpainted bodyshell should now slip over the mounting posts and into position. Adjust the body posts to about the correct height – they can be adjusted more accurately once the body is painted and finished.

The next task is to cut out the body. Most bodies will have trim lines moulded in so that you know where to cut. Either use a sharp pair of scissors to cut the body away from the waste material, or score along the moulded trim lines

tape that will stick well to the bodyshell and prevent paint seepage. To master complex multi-coloured paint schemes the trick is to draw the design on the outside of the bodyshell first using a marker pen, then mask out each of these areas on the inside of the shell. Each of the coloured areas should be thought of as a separate layer: the aim is to paint the darkest areas first, ending with the lightest colour as the final layer. This will ensure the dark colour doesn't bleed through the lighter colours.

These days most shells come with a clear protective covering on the outside, which protects the body from any over-spray during painting and is removed afterwards to reveal a clean and shiny finish. If the shell you're painting doesn't have a protective film you'll have to cover its outer surface with a sheet of newspaper and seal the edges with masking tape.

Painting process

Take your time when spraying the bodyshell, and in order to avoid breathing in the solvent fumes and any overspray always wear a suitable mask and work in a well-ventilated area.

You need to use special paint designed to bond to Lexan polycarbonate. While it's possible to apply this using a paintbrush, a much better finish will be achieved by using either an aerosol or an airbrush. When using an aerosol, make sure that you give it a hard shake for at least two minutes to mix up the paint inside, which may have settled. This will help the paint to spray more consistently.

Before you apply any paint, test each colour on a scrap piece of Lexan to ensure its appearance is as expected (you can use the pieces you cut

ABOVE Here you can see the overspray film that prevents excess spray from getting onto the outside surface of the shell.

FAR LEFT Spend a few minutes shaking the spray can so that the paint mixes well before you apply it to the bodyshell.

LEFT Head outside to avoid breathing in the fumes.

ABOVE Slowly build up the coats of paint, leaving plenty of time in between for each coat to dry.

ABOVE RIGHT You can check for even coverage by holding the shell up to the light.

out for the wheelarches, for instance). That way you'll find out if the paint is too thin or the wrong colour before it's too late! Then apply a thin, consistent coat to the inside of the bodyshell. Leave this to dry, then apply the second coat, a third coat and so on, until a solid colour results. With multiple layers of different colours, this whole process can take a considerable amount of time, but the end results will be well worth the effort. If you have several bodyshells to paint in the same colour scheme, it's a good idea to do them all in the same session.

After each colour has dried, remove the appropriate masking tape from your design and then move on to the next area of the paint

scheme. Once all the colours have been applied and are fully dry, some owners like to add a final backing coat of black, white or silver to the inside of the bodyshell. This adds extra depth to the colours, particularly fluorescent and light ones, as well as making the inside of the shell appear neater. Dark colours look best when backed with silver paint, fluorescent and bright colours are best backed with white, and the reflective qualities of the latest chrome paints are at their best when backed with black.

Finishing touches

When all the paint has dried, the window masks and overspray protective film or tape can be

RIGHT Once painted, the overspray film can be removed.

removed and white spirit can be used to get rid of any sticky residue and pen marks.

Next you cut out and apply the decals as required. With some scale kits it can take as long to apply the decals and finish the body as it took to the build the rest of the car. The results can be impressive, though, and it's possible to end up with a car that looks just like its full-size counterpart. Each decal should be cut out carefully using a sharp model knife or a pair of scissors.

Finally, using the fixings supplied with the bodyshell, attach any extra parts that came with it such as wings or spoilers.

You should now have a great-looking bodyshell that will finish off your new car perfectly and make you the envy of all your friends. If you've expended a lot of effort on it, the first time you take your mini-masterpiece to the race track can be a nerve-wracking experience. For one thing is guaranteed – before long that paintwork will get scratched, so

it's best to just resign yourself to the fact straight away and get on with it. Just take some photos first so that you can look back and admire your handiwork, and then forget about the paintwork and concentrate on your driving. After all, who ever heard of an RC driver racing slowly just to avoid getting a few scuff marks on his car?

ABOVE After the decals have been applied and the shell fitted to the chassis, the result will be well worth the effort.

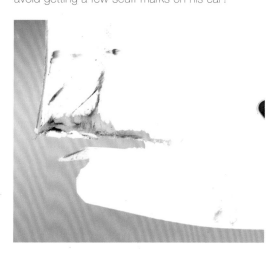

LEFT A ripped or damaged bodyshell is part and parcel of racing, as contact and crashes have to be expected.

Maintaining your car

Keeping your RC model in top
condition   **66**

Prepare a pit area   **67**

Cleaning   **68**

Cleaning nitro-powered cars   **68**

Cleaning electric-powered cars   **71**

Water   **73**

Check the geometry   **74**

Check the electrics   **78**

People preparation   **80**

Keeping your RC model in top condition

Keeping your radio control car operating in tip-top condition demands little more than a few minutes of effort between each run. Regular maintenance will not only help your car run reliably for longer, it will also help to ensure consistent and predictable handling each time you venture onto the racetrack. After each race meeting you'll need to at the very least, clean the air filter (and re-oil), the bodyshell, the chassis and the suspension of any dirt, grease, oil or dust. Use this cleaning session as an opportunity for inspection: look carefully at what you're cleaning and rectify any problems you might find. If your racing included the odd crash here and there, make your checks thorough!

If something doesn't seem to be right, avoid applying quick solutions or making a dodgy temporary repair. Stop, think about the problem, refer back to the kit instructions, or ask someone. When you've found the cause put it right so that it won't happen again, by reassembling to the correct standard, replacing the part, or making a change. Just remember that everyone you talk to had to start the same way as you, and they'll all want to help.

The full extent of the maintenance required will depend on the type of car you own and where you choose to race it. If you drive a micro-sized electric-powered car around the lounge at home you'll be in for a much easier time than if you compete with a nitro-powered off-road car on a slippery, muddy and bumpy circuit. In fact most drivers find that nitro-powered cars provide the ultimate test of their maintenance skills, as the competition finals for these rocket-ships can last as long as 60 minutes. That can be the equivalent of three weeks of club racing with an electric-powered car. When your car has to run reliably for an entire hour it's vitally important to give every component a thorough check before you even get to the track. After all, as the old saying goes, to finish first you first have to finish.

Prepare a pit area

Following the lead of the best full-size racing teams, establishing a clean pit area is the first step towards successful maintenance. Dismantling the car and spreading the parts over an untidy pit table is usually the forerunner to not being able to find a key component when you come to put everything back together. So start by clearing an area on your table and then cover it with a white hand towel. Now whenever you place a component onto the table, not only will the part be easy to see, there's also no danger of it rolling off the table and onto the floor. The towel will also soak up anything you accidentally spill and will save the table from any damage. To further reduce the risk of losing anything important, keep a plastic container next to the towel so that you can place components in it as they come off the car. Differentials and shock absorbers in particular consist of many small parts; an empty ice cream or margarine tub is ideal for ensuring these parts remain together.

If you're cleaning your nitro-powered car at home, do take precautions to avoid dripping fuel onto your carpet. After each run there's almost always some fuel left in the exhaust pipe, so cover

the end of this with a plastic bag secured by an elastic band. While it's relatively easy to clean dirty, sticky fuel off the car, it's much harder to clean it off a woolly carpet!

If you built your car from a kit you'll probably already have a pretty good idea of how everything fits together. If not, keep your instruction booklet to hand. You'll soon discover that dismantling the car is far easier than remembering how to put it all back together again. Whenever in doubt, check the instruction book.

A good set of tools is something you can build up over time, but the absolute minimum requirement for maintenance purposes is all the tools you

ABOVE Working on your car is important if you wish it to finish each race.

OPPOSITE You can learn so much from the top drivers.

BELOW The perfect pit area complete with tools and protective pit mat.
(Upgrade RC)

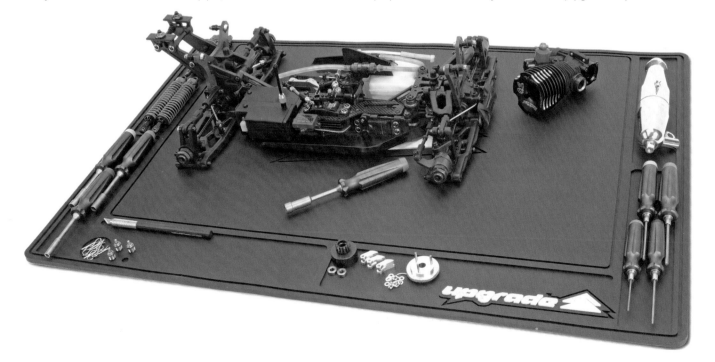

RIGHT A compressor will keep your car clean during the day by blasting off the loose dirt between races.

needed to build the car in the first place. This includes anything that came with the kit itself, such as the Allen keys for the cap-head screws and the T-bar spanner for the nuts. Brushes, a long-nosed pair of pliers, a selection of screwdrivers and a modelling knife are also recommended.

Cleaning

Get into the habit of giving the chassis a quick brush-over or wipe-down after each outing. When the dust and dirt is removed from the car, it's much easier to spot any minor breakages or cracked components. Store your car when it's coated in dirt or moisture and the next time you go to use it parts may have seized or gone rusty. Worse still, it might not work at all.

Some clubs provide access to an air compressor, which is an excellent way to blow most of the dirt off a chassis. Use a stiff brush to dislodge any that's harder to reach before again blowing it away. Sticky residues, such as a mixture of dirt and nitro fuel, can be removed using a rag or strong kitchen towel. Really persistent hard-packed dirt may need to be carefully scraped off using a toothpick or flat-headed screwdriver, taking care not to scratch the chassis. Cotton buds soaked in motor cleaner are ideal for poking into awkward corners. The same cleaner can also be used to wipe the chassis surface clean once the dirt has been removed.

Bodyshells can be dusted down with a brush, or wiped with a rag or kitchen towel if they've got wet. Removing external scuff-marks is best done with a tissue soaked in motor cleaner. Simply rub the scuff-mark vigorously and it will usually come off. Some drivers use furniture polish wipes to put the finishing touches to the shell, leaving the surface gleaming like new.

BELOW Even the inside of a bodyshell gets dirty. You can use a soft brush to remove it without damaging the paint.

Cleaning nitro-powered cars

Nitro cars always seem to end up the messiest. While the simplest way to avoid getting them dirty is to not venture anywhere too messy in the first place, this option is usually the least fun. The nitro fuel itself is a key contributor to the grime. Dirt sticks to it extremely well, so try to avoid splashing any over the chassis when you refill the fuel tank. Check the routing of the exhaust pipe to ensure it doesn't direct any sticky residue directly onto the chassis or bodyshell. If your nitro-powered car is

really dirty, it's a good idea to first remove the engine, fuel tank and exhaust so that you can gain access to all areas of the chassis. Inspect the engine mounts to ensure these are clean since you don't want dirt hindering the transfer of heat from the engine to the chassis.

Cleaning air filters

Since the air filter prevents dirt and dust from getting into the engine, the engine can wear out quickly if the filter isn't working properly. Foam filters can be cleaned by flushing them from behind with compressed air. Remove the filter from the car and spray air through the bottom of the filter holder. Make sure you do this the correct way round so that the air pushes the dirt outwards and not deeper into the filter. Now wash out the air filter in some warm soapy water to remove any remaining debris and leave it to dry. Once dry, re-oil it in accordance with the manufacturer's instructions. If

your car uses a paper filter with pre-filters, the pre-filter should be regularly replaced. The paper filter will then only need to be replaced when you see dirt accumulating in the creases, usually about once per month. However, always replace the paper filter if you accidentally flood the engine and soak the filter with fuel. Even when it fully dries out, a fuel-soaked paper filter won't work properly.

Cleaning fuel tanks

Cleaning the inside of fuel tanks is best done using the fuel itself. Plug the two outlets with fuel tubing, pour some fuel into the tank and then seal the lid. Now shake the fuel around inside the tank for a few minutes and empty it via the outlet hole. Keep repeating this process until you can no longer see any dirt in the tank.

Warm water can be used to clean the outside of the tank, but make sure the tank is appropriately sealed first. Use fuel tubing to connect the pressure

ABOVE LEFT Racing in the wet is a common situation, especially when competing in the UK.
(Adrian Svensson)

ABOVE After you've raced it's time for the hard work to begin.
(Adrian Svensson)

FAR LEFT Wash your air filter out using soapy water. After it has dried fully you can apply fresh air filter oil.

LEFT This fuel tank has been sealed using a piece of fuel pipe and a 3mm screw. It can now be sprayed with cleaner or even washed in soapy water without fear of the liquid getting inside.

ABOVE With the clutch shoes removed you can clean them easier and check for wear.

RIGHT You can clearly see the burr on the edge that needs to be removed.

FAR RIGHT Use a small needle-type file to remove the burr and clean the slot where the clutch spring sits.

fitting to the fuel pickup outlet, to seal the inside of the tank and ensure no water can enter. Then run the tank under warm water and wipe it with a towel. Leave the tank to dry so that any remaining water will evaporate.

Cleaning clutches

Over time, a glaze will form on the clutch; this will develop even quicker if fuel manages to work its way in. Removing this glaze will ensure the clutch works consistently from one run to the next.

To clean the clutch, the engine first has to be removed from the car. Then remove the clutch-bell and the clutch bearings and wipe the inside of the clutch-bell with a clean rag soaked with a suitable fluid, such as brake or motor cleaner. Now use an abrasive cleaning pad to wipe down the inside of

the clutch-bell and scrape off any glaze that's built up on the inside. The abrasive pad can also be used to lightly scrape the glaze off the part of the clutch shoes that contacts the clutch-bell.

Before you put everything back together again, clean, re-oil, and inspect the clutch bearings. Make sure that they operate freely and don't show signs of wear and tear. If they show signs of excessive slop, it's best to replace the bearings rather than run the risk of having them fail during a run.

Cleaning engines

With the engine and exhaust removed from the car, the engine can be sprayed with brake or motor cleaner and wiped clean. Heavily baked residue on the outside of the engine or pipe can be sprayed and then rigorously cleaned with a towel or an old

RIGHT Often a nitro engine will be supplied with caps that can be used to seal the engine for cleaning.

FAR RIGHT Using motor cleaner and a toothbrush, you can blast off the dirt that gets ingrained during the course of a race meeting.

LEFT Cleaning your electric car after a race in these conditions will take time and effort.

toothbrush. When the engine's dry, remove the glow plug and air filter and drip a few drops of after-run oil into the glow plug hole. Then clean and re-oil the air filter. Finally, tug the pull-starter to cycle the engine, and replace the plug and air filter.

Fitting a new glow plug before a major final can be a good idea, but make sure you leave enough time to tune the engine again. The impact can be minimised by ensuring the glow plug you install is the same make and model as the one you've just removed. For a one-hour final, a slightly richer needle setting will help prevent the engine from overheating or stopping during the race.

ABOVE You'll need to strip down a brushless motor so that you can carry out maintenance.

Cleaning electric-powered cars

How frequently you need to rebuild an electric motor depends on the type of motor that's fitted in your car. Brushless motors require by far the least maintenance, followed by brushed stock motors, and then brushed modified motors. Start by cleaning the outside of the motor with a brush or a cleaning rag and then inspect it for any obvious signs of damage or wear.

Brushless motor maintenance

With no brushes to replace and no commutator to re-cut, the number of maintenance tasks is dramatically reduced with a brushless motor. Of course, there's no such thing as a maintenance-

LEFT Although brushless motors are virtually maintenance-free the bearings will still need to be lubricated using suitable light oil.

RIGHT By removing the endbell on a brushed motor you'll be able to see how the commutator has worn.

free motor, but brushless systems do come very close. The motor needs to be kept clean, the wires must be in good working order, and you'll need to occasionally lightly oil the two main motor bearings. This means you don't require any motor cleaner spray, brush drops, replacement brushes, springs or a motor lathe, all of which saves money in the long term.

Brushless motors don't provide a lot of resistance when you spin the armature by hand, so with the motor dusted down and removed from the car you can quickly check for any stickiness. If you sense that it's not spinning as freely as it should, you should disassemble the motor and clean it. In particular, the partially exposed main bearing needs to spin as freely as possible, so after cleaning you should apply a drop or two of thin bearing lubricant.

Brushed motor maintenance

With a brushed motor, the general rule is that the more frequently you rebuild it the better. By skimming the commutator after every other race, you'll only need to make a few small cuts with a motor lathe to return the shiny surface to the copper. Wait for ten races or more and the poor electrical contact and subsequent arcing between the brushes and the commutator will have caused more damage, leaving the commutator with a blackened or scored surface. Many more cuts with a lathe are then required to remove the mess. Long periods between motor rebuilds also means that its performance will gradually deteriorate. With a modified motor you might notice the drop-off in performance after just a couple of runs. Stock motors can be raced somewhat more before the reduction becomes noticeable.

If you have a brushed motor, always keep a close watch on the motor brushes and replace them when necessary. They should definitely be

BELOW Before putting the brushed motor back together, give it a good spray with motor cleaner to remove any dirt or loose copper from the commutator after it's been cut.

BELOW RIGHT On the brushed motor's endbell you can see the capacitors that suppress the unwanted noise that can cause erratic performance during use.

replaced whenever they're excessively worn or show any discolouring. If the brushes look fine you may be able to clean the surface and then run them again, but if you skim the motor commutator at the same time you'll still have to break the brushes in again, as the diameter of the commutator will have changed.

Many unwanted radio frequencies are generated by the motor in an electric car. In a brushed motor, as the motor brushes bounce up and down on the rotating commutator they generate radio frequencies that can affect the receiver. To suppress these signals, small ceramic capacitors are soldered to the motor's endbell. On some modified motors these come pre-installed; on others they'll be included in the packet and require soldering into position. Use a hot soldering iron to do this, and keep the capacitor legs as short as possible to ensure they don't catch on the chassis when the motor is installed. Whenever you remove the motor from the car, check the capacitors to

ensure they remain firmly soldered in place. A dry solder joint on one of the legs can be enough to give the car major radio interference. Many high-frequency speed controls also require a Schottky diode to be fitted that further isolates high voltage spikes.

Water

Water is the main enemy of electrical components, so the objective is to prevent the two from coming into contact. Many nitro-powered cars are now supplied with sealed plastic covers for their radio equipment. Competition-orientated cars often offer a moulded plastic cover for the chassis to seal it from the elements and ensure minimal water and dirt works its way inside. Sometimes these are available as an aftermarket item. Even with such a cover fitted, however, it's still a good idea to thoroughly waterproof the electrical components. Many different techniques can be used.

Some drivers insert the components into a balloon and seal the neck with a tie-wrap. For electric-powered cars, many manufacturers now market speed controls that are already waterproofed. Some specialist companies will even waterproof a receiver for you by encasing the electrics in a plastic resin. If, despite your best efforts, any electrics do get wet, remove them from the car immediately and put them somewhere warm to dry. The airing cupboard at home is an ideal place. Leave the components there for a day

and the water will evaporate. With any luck the item will then start working again.

It is always better to invest time in removing damp and dirt and thoroughly lubricating all of the moving parts than to leave a car covered in mud. Rust can build up within a few hours and it doesn't require much of it to seize the small hinges and linkages on an RC car. A spray-can of WD-40 is a handy way to quickly prevent rust from building up on the gearbox, shock shafts, axles, steering links and suspension hinges. However, to prevent metal parts from rusting you need to reapply oil and grease.

Don't leave fuel in the tank between race

ABOVE Water and electrical components don't mix, so many manufacturers offer a sealed box into which the radio components can be installed for protection.

BELOW Use a balloon over receivers to keep the water out. This is a cheap and simple preventative measure.

ABOVE If you have to run in the wet you can apply some GT85, which contains PTFE to protect the metal parts from rusting.

ABOVE RIGHT A range of cleaners that are friendly to the chassis and suspension components.

BELOW Place you car on a perfectly flat surface so that it can be checked over in detail.

meetings either. Nitro fuel attracts moisture from the air, so leaving fuel in the engine and fuel tubes is a sure way to steer that moisture to the most expensive component in the truck. Draining the fuel from the tank and running the engine dry helps to prevent such corrosion from occurring.

Check the geometry

Once the car's been cleaned, your attention should turn to checking for breakages or worn parts and then checking the geometry. Use a hand-operated screwdriver, not an electric one, to confirm that each screw remains tight. Metal-to-metal fasteners, such as the engine-mounting screws, will benefit from having a drop of blue compound Loctite

added before the screw is tightened. Then check for loose or worn steering rod ends, suspension arms, linkages or bulkheads. If something looks suspect, it's always a good idea to replace it to reduce the chance of it failing during a race. Also check the servo horns for small cracks and ensure the servo mounting screws remain tight.

Since adjustments of just a few millimetres are sufficient to change the handling of a car it's worth confirming between each run that everything remains appropriately aligned. Some fairly elementary measuring tools are sufficient to check most settings, which you can either purchase or construct yourself.

Check for tweak

For a radio control car to handle consistently, it requires the same amount of weight to be placed on the left-hand and right-hand sides. If more weight sits on one side than the other, then the car will pull to that side when the throttle is opened. This difference in weight distribution is often referred to as 'tweak', and can be caused by a number of different factors including a twisted chassis, unequal-length shock absorbers, uneven droop screw settings, or inconsistent settings of the shock absorber collars. There are many measuring tools available that will help you check for tweak. The most sophisticated allow the corner weights of the car to be accurately measured, confirming that the static weight distribution is entirely appropriate.

To check for chassis tweak, you need to remove the wheels and the battery straps and then place the car on a perfectly flat surface, such as a chassis set-up board. If the chassis rocks from side-to-side or from back-to-front, then the chassis

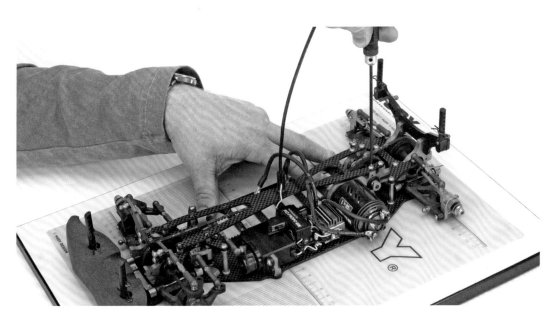

LEFT Tweak in an on-road car will make it inconsistent to drive. By loosening off all the screws in the top deck you can check that there's no tweak in the chassis as you tighten them up again, one at a time.

BELOW LEFT Using a set of callipers to check that the preload on the shocks is the same left to right. This may change, though, if the car is tweaked, as these are adjusted independently to eliminate the tweak effect.

BELOW This is an MIP Tweak Station. Looking at the bubble in the middle indicates whether there's more load on one side than the other. By adjusting the threaded collars on the shock the loadings can be changed until the bubble sits perfectly central.

is twisted. The way to fix this depends on your type of chassis. If there's an upper and lower chassis deck, undoing the screws on the top deck, pushing the lower deck onto the flat surface, and then pinching the top deck screws tight again, will typically fix the problem. If you have a one-piece moulded chassis, then removing any obvious twist may require a whole new chassis to be fitted.

If the chassis is flat, any remaining tweak will be caused by the suspension settings. To confirm this, measure and mark the centre of the car's chassis at the front and rear. Then place the car on a completely flat surface and, using the tip of a modelling knife blade placed directly beneath the mark you've just made, lift one end of the chassis until both wheels are clear of the ground, and slowly lower it back down. Both tyres should touch

the surface at the same time. If they don't, then the suspension is tweaked.

If your car allows the suspension droop to be altered, first check that the droop screws on each corner have the same setting. A droop gauge can be used to do this. Different droop screw settings will have the same effect as different length shock absorbers and will cause the car to roll more round some corners than others. The amount of left and right droop needs to be identical, but the amount of front and rear droop can be different.

The next thing to check is whether the shock absorber on the left of the car is the same length as the one on the right. Use a Vernier gauge to do this. Finally, check the position of the threaded collars or the number of plastic shock spacers. Ideally the shock absorbers need to feel equally

RIGHT A camber gauge is a cheap tool that can be used to measure the angle of your wheels. Off-road cars tend to run a little more negative camber (where the top of the tyre points inwards) than this on-road touring car chassis that runs a single degree.

firm. Assuming both shock absorbers have the same amount of oil in them, the tension on the spring is the area to adjust. If the right-hand tyre touches down before the left-hand, you can either increase the preload of the left-hand tyre by winding down the collar slightly, or decrease the preload on the right-hand spring by winding the collar up.

Note that even though the quality of today's RC cars is extremely high, the differences in shock absorber size and mouldings may require the collar settings to be slightly different on each corner. However, if this difference is more than about 1mm it suggests that the tweak might more likely be caused by a twisted chassis.

BELOW To adjust the toe-in at the front of your car, view it from above. More toe-in will make the car easier to drive but will affect its top speed. A car with a little toe-out will be more aggressive on turn-in.

Check the suspension

The suspension arms need to be able to move up and down freely. To check this, remove all the wheels, anti-roll bars and shock absorbers and then place the car onto a stand so that everything is clear of the table surface. Now lift one of the suspension arms. When you let it go it should fall freely. If it sticks on the way down, you'll need to clean or replace the suspension arm pins or the arm itself to solve the problem.

Check the camber

Camber is the angle between vertical and a line passing down the middle of each wheel. The camber is said to be negative when the top of the wheel leans in towards to the car and positive when it leans out. Camber helps to ensure the tyre contact patch is kept as large as possible at all times when the car is on the track. Using a camber gauge, it will only take a few seconds to confirm the settings are the same on both sides. When set at normal ride height most cars will have a camber setting of between 0 and 2°.

Check the toe-in

The term 'toe-in' describes a pair of wheels that are angled closer together at the front than at the rear when viewed from above. The opposite is called 'toe-out'. As with camber, most cars work best with a maximum of 2° of toe-in or toe-out. The instruction manual should confirm the recommended setting for your car, so your task is simply to confirm that the actual settings match the advice provided.

Check the ride height

As a car hurtles round the track its shock absorbers move up and down to absorb the bumps, and the ride height determines how effective this movement is in keeping the chassis clear of the ground. The higher the ride, the more it will roll during cornering. Go too high and it may flip over completely. This is particularly noticeable when competing on a very high traction surface such as carpet, where a ride height adjustment of just a few millimetres can make the difference between cornering quickly and making a speedy exit into the scenery. Setting the ride height too low will prevent the suspension from handling the bumps and the car will become very nervous as it strikes the ground. The ride height should therefore always be raised when racing on very bumpy surfaces.

A flat surface is needed to measure the ride height. A sheet of thick glass or wood is ideal. Push the car down on its suspension and then insert a suitable measuring gauge under each corner. If you don't have a gauge use some coins. Measure the thickness of the coin and then see if it slips under the car. Add another coin and try again. When the coins touch the chassis, try them under the other three corners and adjust the ride height accordingly so that all four corners are the same. Adjustments are made by inserting small plastic spacers above the shock absorber spring. Different widths of spacer are supplied in most kits. More expensive kits may be supplied with threaded shock absorber collars that are wound up and down to perform the same task.

Check the differentials

With a two-wheel-drive on-road chassis, the setting of the rear limited slip differential is crucial to ensuring that the car will exit the corner in a straight line. It can also affect the way a four-wheel-drive car accelerates out of a bend.

A differential aids cornering by allowing the wheel on the outside of a corner to travel faster than the wheel on the inside. In doing so, it prevents the inside wheels from being dragged round the circuit, as this would quickly wear out tyres and make the car less precise to drive. Differentials usually require very little maintenance if they've been set up in accordance with the manufacturer's instructions. However, after a while they may develop a 'gritty' feeling, caused by dust entering the sealed unit. A rebuild of the differential is then required.

As a general rule you're much less likely to notice the effect of a sticking differential on a high traction circuit, where the differentials can be set tight. But on slippery or bumpy surfaces, where differentials are often set loose to help distribute the

power between the wheels, a 'sticky diff' will cause the car to pull to one side under acceleration. Remove the unit from the car and perform a rebuild whenever you detect that the movement of the differentials is not as smooth as it should be. Sometimes it's just a matter of removing the dust from the unit. Silicone-filled gear differentials require the gears to be cleaned thoroughly before fresh silicone oil is applied.

For ball differentials, the differential rings and balls need to be cleaned and re-lubricated. Occasionally you'll need to replace worn parts such as the rings or the tiny balls that run on them. Most manufacturers sell differential rebuild kits specifically for this purpose.

ABOVE There are tools available to help you tension an adjustable ball-type differential.

BELOW With your ball-type differential taken apart, you should replace the diff rings if they're scored. The diff balls, on the other hand, won't need to be replaced as frequently.

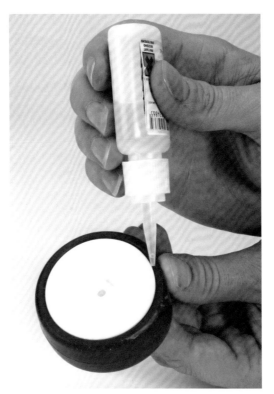

RIGHT If a tyre starts to come away from the rim, pull it back and place a drop of glue into the gap. Then let the tyre go but hold it in position against the rim until the glue dries.

RIGHT Unlike a rubber tyre, as a foam tyre is used its diameter is reduced. Here you can clearly see how a foam tyre from a touring car has worn over a series of races and has become coned in shaped due to running with negative camber.

RIGHT Due to its make-up, a foam tyre is susceptible to damage in use. 'Chunking' is when a chunk of foam is ripped out of the tyre's surface when it comes into contact with the bodyshell, for example in a crash.

Check the tyres

Foam tyres aren't as common as they once were, but they're frequently still used when racing indoors, particularly when a carpet track surface is used. While they provide excellent traction they also require regular maintenance, as very rarely do all four tyres wear at the same rate. Unless you adopt a rigorous routine of swapping the tyres round after every race, before long you'll end up with larger tyres on one side than the other, and then handling problems can start. Since the diameter of the tyre affects the gearing of the car, it now effectively has different gearing on each side. One side will therefore attempt to spin its wheels faster than the other side and thereby put the differentials under load. The handling can then become unpredictable, with the car behaving differently around left-hand and right-hand bends. The simple cure with foam tyres is to always true them again before the next race to ensure the diameters remain identical. However, this is a messy process and requires a dedicated tyre truing machine. This will enable you to eliminate coning or flat spots, although the diameter of the tyre will be reduced as a result.

With moulded rubber tyres, the tyre diameter remains largely unchanged regardless of wear, and it's how well the tyre's been glued to the wheel that primarily dictates how accurately the car will accelerate. Assuming that the wheels on both sides are the same size and have the same tyre insert and rubber compound, the most likely reason for unpredictable handling will be if one of the tyres has started to separate from the wheel. This will cause the tyre to swell under acceleration, altering both the size of the tyre contact patch and the gearing on that side of the car. For this reason it's important to always check the tyres between each run to ensure they remain firmly glued to the wheels. A small drop of superglue should be applied whenever a gap is detected. Even the smallest of gaps can grow bigger once subjected to the enormous sideways forces that tyres have to contend with on the track.

Check the electrics

Check the transmitter and receiver batteries

Your radio gear must always be in good working order as it's the only connection between you and the car. Always ensure that the transmitter has charged batteries. Most transmitters have a dial or health-check meter that allows you to monitor how much power remains. If your transmitter came with non-rechargeable (dry) AA batteries, it's a good idea

LEFT If you're using regular AA cells like these, keep an eye on their status. This is usually shown by a set of LEDs on the front of the transmitter. If in any doubt replace them to prevent you from losing control.

to replace these at the earliest opportunity with a suitable set of rechargeable cells and an accompanying charger. Not only does this work out as a far cheaper option long-term, but you now have the ability to give the cells a fresh charge between races, which is essential if you race in a class with long finals, such as the larger scale off-road and on-road classes.

Nitro-powered cars and some electric-powered cars also use a high capacity on-board battery to power the receiver or radio gear. Again, make sure this battery is fully charged. Losing battery power from your car or transmitter before the race finishes is not an experience you'll want to repeat too often.

Check the transmitter trims

Keeping your transmitter in a padded box or carry-case between races is a good way to protect it from any unnecessary knocks. Unless a transmitter has digital trims, a small nudge may be all it takes to move one of the tiny levers and change the throttle or steering settings. Since the front wheels only need to be fractionally off-centre for the car to pull to one side under acceleration, always perform a simple straight-line check once you get to the track. To do this, place the car on a completely flat section of the circuit and slowly drive it forwards using just the throttle control, watching to confirm whether it tracks in a straight line. If the car drifts to the right, move the trim lever on the transmitter to the left to

BELOW LEFT The trim is the small adjustment below the transmitter stick shown here. It can often get knocked during transportation.

BELOW With this type of transmitter some of the settings are digital so cannot be adjusted whilst the unit is turned off.

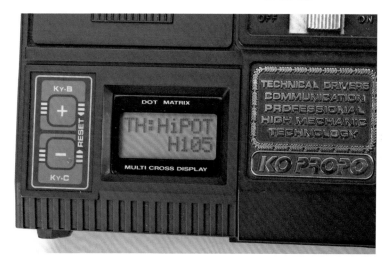

RIGHT By purchasing a dedicated bag or case you can protect your investment and save it from getting damaged or knocked.

bring it back into a straight line. Then perform the check again. After two or three short runs you should have found a trim setting that enables the car to track straight. At the top level you'll see drivers performing these checks before each race, making short practice runs to adjust the steering trim setting before the car is placed on the starting grid.

On odd occasions the required trim setting might fall between two clicks on the transmitter lever. If you have a digital trim you may be able to compensate for this by adjusting its finer setting. Alternatively, it may prove necessary to get a screwdriver out and reposition the servo saver on

the servo arm. Moving this by one notch may be all that's necessary to find a better position. You'll also need to do this if the trim lever on the transmitter is left at the extremes of its movement once the ideal trim setting has been found.

Check the servo end-points too. These are adjusted to ensure the steering is never moved over so far that the wheels bind up or hit the suspension arms. In doing so, it not only prevents the front wheels from locking up in tight corners, but it also ensures the servo isn't placed under undue load and thereby saves the servo motor from burning out. Many transmitters now come with end-point adjustment (EPA) functionality. For the steering, this allows a car's turning circle to be set to be the same arc regardless of whether it's turning left or right. On nitro-powered cars EPA can be used to precisely adjust the servo travel for the throttle and brake, all without having to change the neutral point of the servo. When adjusted correctly it can eliminate the need for overload protection springs.

Check the wires

Intermittent electrical contact can generate power spikes and cause glitches, so check all leads to ensure that soldered connections are firm and won't break apart when the wire is given a quick tug. Then check the connectors themselves to ensure they fit together securely and don't shake about. The plugs into the receiver are prime candidates to check, particularly when mixing the receiver and servos from different manufacturers. If any wires show signs of cuts or fraying, replace them. Use electrical tape to insulate and secure any wires that are exposed or at risk of contacting one another.

People preparation

Get your maintenance tasks out of the way well before your next race so that there's no last-minute panic. That will leave you with time to prepare yourself and, if you're competing in a nitro-powered race, your pit-person.

Pit stops are an exciting part of the race when competing with a nitro-powered car. The driver has to remain on the rostrum, so it's the pit-person who has to do the hard work, solving technical problems and adding fuel to the screaming machine. That makes your pit-person an essential part of your race strategy. You must ensure they have a good understanding of how your car works and can deal with small maintenance tasks during the race. Being able to restart the car if the engine cuts out is a vital skill, along with the ability to refuel it and fit new tyres quickly.

Before the race, be sure to provide your pit-person

RIGHT With more complex radios you can adjust how far the steering travels. You should always set the end-points on a transmitter if you have the option, as it stops the servos from straining and potential internal damage.

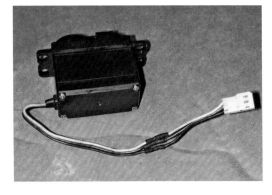

RIGHT If you have a broken or damaged wire it's best to remake the joint and then place some heatshrink over the connection.

FAR LEFT A cheap plastic tub like this is useful at a race meeting to carry your equipment from the pit area to the pit lane. You can also use it to hold spares and useful tools.

with a small collection of tools and parts, including extra fuel, an engine tuning screwdriver, glow plug wrench and spare glow plug, a starter box, needle-nose pliers and a spare set of tyres. They should then be fully prepared for most eventualities.

Also be sure to brief your pit-person on your intended race strategy before the event starts. Tell them when you intend to come into the pits and agree on the signal the pit-person will use when they want you to come into the pit lane. If you don't do this before the race begins, you'll find it can get pretty chaotic as you attempt to shout to each other over the noise of the race cars!

PIT STOP SEQUENCE ONE – the person in the pit lane shouts to tell his driver that it's time to come in for fuel.

PIT STOP SEQUENCE TWO – getting ready to receive the car.

PIT STOP SEQUENCE THREE – the pit-person holds up his arm so that the driver knows where to stop.

PIT STOP SEQUENCE FOUR – in one fluid motion, the car is picked up and placed on the pit lane wall to aid refuelling.

PIT STOP SEQUENCE FIVE – the fuel goes in using a special gun that speeds up the process.

PIT STOP SEQUENCE SIX – the car is quickly returned to the track and is driven from the pit lane at speed.

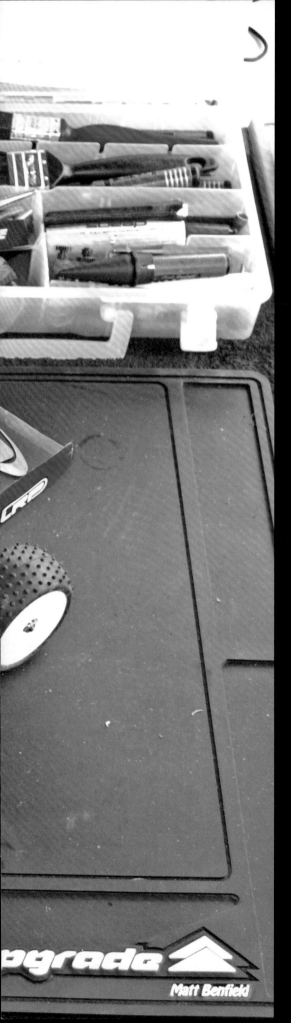

Performance enhancements

Upgrading your RC model	84
Upgrading electrics	86
Batteries	88
Changing chassis settings	95
Setting the suspension	100
Gearing it right	103
Bodyshells	105
Wheels and tyres	106
Drifting	107

Upgrading your RC model

One of the really great things about radio control model car racing is that there's always so much to learn. To become successful you need to become a one-person race team, an expert in chassis set up, tyre choice, engine maintenance and suspension tuning. Then, to top it all, you have to drive the car as well!

ABOVE There are plenty of 'go faster' items you can spend your money on.

Spend, or change the set-up?

There are two ways to enhance the performance of your model car. One way is to spend some money and upgrade parts; the other is to make set-up changes to alter its handling characteristics. When it comes to making set-up adjustments, how much scope you have will depend on the type of car you purchased in the first place. Many introductory cars are deliberately engineered with few set-up options, since the manufacturer wants to ensure all cars will deliver sensible performance. Given a wide choice of set-up, it's just as easy to turn a car into an evil-handling beast as a corner-hugging race winner. For most models, a wide range of hop-up parts is available from the original manufacturer or from third-party tune-up specialists. Some parts may make your car go faster in a straight line; others are aimed at increasing cornering speed,

ABOVE Just look at the abundance of blue alloy components fitted to this Tamiya chassis. *(Ian Lloyd)*

BELOW LEFT A system like this Team Orion one can be used during your own testing.

BELOW By installing a timing system such as those from Robitronic or AMB (shown in the photograph) you can make sure that the upgrades and changes are making a difference to your lap times.

jumping prowess, or reliability. Other hop-up parts are there just to make your car look better.

Perfecting the handling of an RC car is mainly achieved through lots and lots of practice, but test sessions can be made much more meaningful and productive by the additional application of a little theory. Understanding the likely effect of any adjustment allows handling to be predicted before the car even hits the track. Not only does this save plenty of time when testing, should you choose to enter competitions it will prove to be

an essential skill on race day. Knowing how to adjust a car to match ever-changing track conditions is a skill that really does separate the winners from the losers.

When adjustments of a couple of millimetres can affect the handling it also helps to be able to measure accurately. Most settings can be adjusted by eye, but this is a highly inaccurate method compared to the use of a proper set of measuring equipment. In fact, some fairly elementary measuring tools will prove sufficient for

ABOVE Adjusting the shock collars by just a single turn can make a huge difference on track.

BELOW Upgrading your electric motor will result in an immediate speed increase.

most adjustments – tools that you can purchase or construct yourself. Alternatively, if you're prepared to invest, most of the tools can be bought together as a complete 'set-up station'. Ensuring that all measurements are taken from a flat surface is particularly important. Suitable set-up boards are available for this, or you can construct your own from a sheet of thick glass or a piece of kitchen worktop.

Upgrading electrics

If you race an electric car, an obvious first step to going faster is to upgrade the electrics. You have an initial choice to make here: do you want to use a brushed motor or a brushless motor? Your choice will largely determine the type of speed control you'll require to regulate the power.

Brushed stock motors

Most starter kits come with a brushed stock motor, and these are an excellent choice both for beginners and for drivers who enjoy close racing. The performance offered by stock motors tends to be very similar and the sensible levels of power they provide not only makes them much less dependent on the quality of battery packs, but they're also less fussy about the set-up of your chassis. Even if the handling of your car isn't quite right, you should still be able to lap consistently using a stock motor.

The stock motors provided in entry-level kits are perfectly adequate for use at home. However, they're usually not designed to be taken apart, so there's not a lot you can do to keep them in good working order. Eventually they'll slow down and will have to be replaced. By the time you start competing at club level, owning a motor you can dismantle and maintain is therefore a far better choice. Rebuildable stock motors conform to a strict set of rules established by the sport's governing bodies, allowing different manufacturers to build motors that provide similar amounts of power. To keep the price down, adjustment options are limited to help ensure that every driver enjoys similar performance.

Different types of stock motor are popular across the globe. In Europe, 27-turn stock and 19-turn super stock are the popular types, their names denoting the number of turns of wire that

are wound round the armature stack. In Asia, 23-turn stock motors are very popular.

Brushed modified motors

Brushed modified motors are ball-raced, offer adjustable timing, and have interchangeable armatures with different winds of wire available to alter the characteristics of the motor. Generally the fewer winds a motor has, the more revs it will pull, making the car feel livelier on the throttle. But the choice of wind has to be balanced against the available battery duration, so on very large tracks a milder wind can sometimes be a better choice since it will drain less power from the battery pack.

Before changing to a more powerful brushed motor, you first need to ensure your speed control – or ESC, as it's commonly referred to – is capable of regulating the power. Not only is it dangerous to fry an ESC due to an excessive current load, but it can also be very expensive! If your electric car uses a mechanical type of control, typically a wiper-board or rotary-coil, then you should definitely replace it. An electronic speed control will greatly improve the accuracy of your throttle control, should hopefully prove to be maintenance free, and will provide much longer run times. Since it replaces the mechanical speed control, the throttle servo and the battery pack that power the radio equipment, an ESC is much lighter too and it will enable your car to be fitted with a more powerful motor. If you still crash regularly, opt for a reasonably priced speed control that has reverse fitted. If not, choose a forward-only version that can handle the highest horsepower motors. When selecting a speed

ABOVE Substituting a worn-out stock motor with a brand-new one will see a performance increase, as would replacing used brushes.

LEFT An example of a modified motor from Checkpoint.

FAR LEFT Upgrading from a mechanical speed control will offer huge benefits.

LEFT Some electronic speed control units have restrictions on the motor's performance whilst others, such as this Novak version, will cater for both brushed and brushless motors.

cylindrical magnet is much lighter than a traditional rotating armature, being made from a one-piece 'rare earth' material that provides a better magnetic field. The lighter rotating mass allows the motor to accelerate faster and with much less vibration than a conventional brushed motor, providing very smooth throttle control and lots of torque. The downside of brushless motor systems is that their initial cost is higher than equivalent brushed motor technology.

Most brushless motors are sold as a set with a matching electronic speed control. Some of the speed controls will even work with a brushed motor should you decide to switch between the two.

ABOVE A range of brushless motors is available to suit the application and track conditions.

control, do check out the after-sales arrangements, just in case something does go wrong. Knowing that any repairs can be completed within a few days is much more reassuring than finding out that the control has to be mailed overseas.

Brushless motors

A brushless motor is like a conventional brushed motor but turned inside out: the coils on the outside are stationary, while the magnets are on the rotor and rotate. The clever bit is the microprocessor technology and software used to control the excitation of the electromagnetic coils. This system continually monitors the position of the rotor and controls the motor timing.

The brushless design provides a number of advantages. Since the windings are stationary and located on the outside of the motor, they're next to the external airflow. As a result the motor operates at a lower temperature, which improves efficiency and results in longer run times. Also, the rotating

BELOW Over the last few years battery technology has improved tremendously. *(LRP Electronic)*

Batteries

Electric-powered radio control cars use an onboard rechargeable battery pack to provide the energy for both the main drive motor and the radio gear. The size and number of cells allowed in an RC car battery is regulated by the sport's governing bodies, who limit it to six commercially available 1.2V sub-C sized cells. These cells are able to deliver a very high current for short periods of time, enabling them to power very fast electric motors. Their mille-ampere hour rating (mAh) indicates how much energy they're capable of storing, often referred to as their capacity.

Nickel Cadmium (NiCd) rechargeable cells were used in RC cars for many years. Their capacity doubled between 1980 and 2000, enabling cars to go faster and race for longer. However, following concerns over the long-term environmental unfriendliness of such cells, Nickel-Metal Hydride (NiMH) technology has taken over. Since NiMH cells provide even more capacity than the old NiCd cells, it hasn't taken much effort to convince top drivers of the need to change – after all, every driver likes a car that can go even faster!

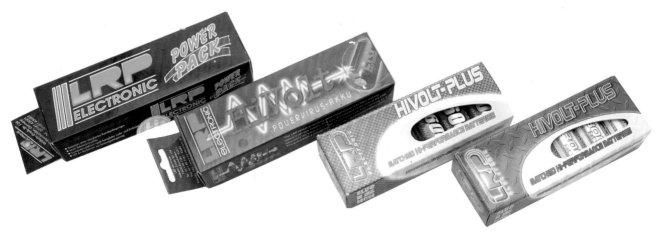

LEFT An example of NiCd cells being selected at the Team Orion factory in Switzerland. *(Team Orion)*

In addition, unlike NiCd cells the NiMH variety can be safely used many times in one race meeting with no obvious loss in performance, as long as they're allowed to cool down completely before being placed on charge again.

The cheapest battery packs come pre-assembled in a shrink-wrapped, stick pack configuration, with a plug fitted suitable for use with starter kits. The capacity of such packs may be quite low – 1,300mAh is a typical rating. Compare this with a competition battery pack of 3,000mAh or more and it's immediately obvious that the cheaper battery packs are only intended for use with low-powered motors. They'll work with a modified motor, but the car will only run at speed for a couple of minutes before it starts to slow down. If you're intending to race at a local club, then 2,000mAh cells and above are the best choice. With a sensible motor and gearing your car will then be capable of lasting a full five-minute race.

The ultimate performance comes when six similar cells with high capacity and voltage are put together to make a competition race pack. To create these, distributors use sophisticated computer systems that repeatedly charge and discharge large numbers of cells at once. Recordings are made of the performance of each individual cell, and the computer then matches similar cells together. Because of this process, such packs are often called 'computer-matched' batteries. The very best battery packs, those with the most punch and duration, may actually never make it into the model shops for someone to buy. The distributors will typically put them to one side for use by their sponsored team drivers at major race events such as the IFMAR World Championship.

LEFT Stick packs are supplied with an industry-standard Tamiya-style connector to make it easy to plug in and go.

LEFT Matching companies invest thousands in computer-controlled machines to ensure that the customer gets the best packs. *(Team Orion)*

ABOVE Building battery packs takes patience and a few specialist tools.

Building battery packs

Computer-matched competition cells are usually sold in loose packs of six and therefore have to be soldered together before they can be used. Care has to be taken when doing this as a bad soldering job may not only result in the pack looking awful, but can also reduce the performance of the cells, particularly if they get too hot. But if you follow eight simple steps the task can be completed successfully:

Choose the tools – A high quality soldering iron is needed, one that will easily heat all of the components at once. A battery jig is the easiest

RIGHT A decent soldering iron, battery jig and solder will make the job of constructing a battery pack out of loose cells a whole lot easier.

LEFT You can now 'tin' both ends of each cell.

way to ensure the cells are properly aligned and a great way to avoid dropping solder on your fingers. Long-nosed pliers are also invaluable to avoid burning your hands. Add the battery bars, connectors and solder and you'll have all you need, but for a really first-class job some clear heat-shrink wrap, a pair of scissors and a hair-dryer are also recommended.

Shrink-wrap the cells – A great way to ensure your cells always remain in good condition, and to protect them from shorting out on your chassis, is to slide a piece of clear shrink-wrap over each cell. Cut it to size and then blast it with a hair-dryer to shrink it over the labels and give you a perfectly protected cell.

Scuff the ends – Use a small piece of 'wet and dry' paper to scuff up the ends of the cells. The rough surface will make the solder stick far better and will help to ensure it ends up in exactly the right place.

Tin the ends – Ensure your soldering iron gets nice and hot before you take it anywhere near the cells. The aim is to keep the iron on the cells for the shortest time possible, since excessive heat can damage them. First 'tin' both ends of each cell with some high quality silver solder.

Use the jig – Decide how you want the pack of cells to sit in your car. If a stick pack is needed, then the cells will sit together in one line, but think about which end you want the positive terminal to be at. For saddle packs, the positive terminal is normally kept closest to the speed control. Lay the cells out in the assembly jig so that the positive

BELOW With the ends of the cells 'tinned' you can get ready to solder the bars into position.

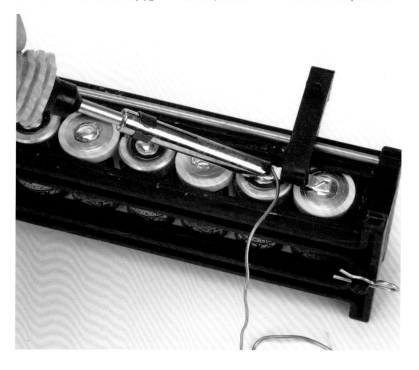

ABOVE Thin-nose pliers will prevent your fingers from burning when you're fitting the connectors.

ABOVE RIGHT Remember to connect the charger wires to the correct ends of the battery pack.

BELOW An alternative to a 12V battery is a regulated mains power supply.

terminals will be soldered to the negative ones, taking care not to accidentally fit one of the cells the wrong way round. For that added touch of professionalism, ensure all the labels are facing upwards too.

Hold the bar – Use a pair of long-nose pliers to hold a battery bar across each pair of cells and push it down onto the terminals. Hold the soldering iron on one side of the bar and feed some solder onto the top. Quickly put down the solder after you've applied it, and use the pliers to hold the bar down while you remove the tip of the iron. Hopefully you'll have a nice clean join. When you've completed one side of the bar, follow the same procedure for the other side, and then for the rest of the pack. Watch out when you flip the

pack over to do the other side, though – you don't want to fix a bar across two cells that you've already connected! If you're making a saddle pack, cut a length of thick flexible wire that's long enough to span the gap in the chassis and use this to connect the two halves of the pack together.

Add the connectors – Most racers choose to fit connectors onto their cells. For starter packs a single plug is often used, while competition races are likely to use 'tube' connectors. These can be a little tricky to solder into place, but tin them first and then let the solder flow smoothly down the length of the bar. Put one on the positive terminal, one on the negative terminal, and then mark which is which on the cell label. Connecting a pack of cells the wrong way round is an experience you quickly learn not to repeat.

Glue them together – An optional step is to glue the cells together with a small dab of superglue. A tiny drop between the cells will be sufficient to ensure they stay together and won't break apart in the event of a heavy impact. If you've put some clear heat-shrink around the cells as recommended above, breaking them apart is then simply a matter of tearing this wrapper away, leaving you with a bunch of brand-new-looking batteries.

Battery charging

To charge a battery pack, the energy has to be transferred from somewhere else. Although some chargers are available that plug into a mains supply, the majority are designed to connect to a 12V battery such as that found in a car or

LEFT With this Robitronic charger you can see the temperature probe connected to the middle of the battery pack.

caravan. This must be fully charged before the charger is connected and should always be stored in a plastic container to prevent it from falling over and spilling harmful acid. The battery pack must always be connected via a suitable charger too – it's extremely dangerous to ever connect the cells straight to a 12V battery.

There are four different ways to charge a battery pack from a 12V battery. Whichever method is used, you must be sure not to not overcharge the cells, and must always disconnect them immediately if they get really hot – if you don't the cells may start to vent, forcing gas out through small holes in the casing. This will permanently damage the battery's capacity. Try to time the charge of your cells so that you can use them shortly after the charging process has finished. If you're unable to do this, charge the cells early and then re-peak them on the charger shortly before your race.

Manual charging – Some starter kits will come with a charge lead that consists of two crocodile clips, a small plug and a large resistor. The charging process is started by attaching the two large clips to the 12V battery (black to negative, red to positive) and then plugging the other end of the lead into the battery pack. It will take between 20 and 45 minutes to charge the cells, depending on their capacity. When they become warm to touch, the lead must be disconnected and the cells can then be clipped into the car.

The big disadvantage of this charging method is that it requires the temperature of the cells to be continually checked. Forget to do so, perhaps through chatting with friends, and there's a real risk that the cells may be overcharged and damaged. Leave the cells connected for too long and they may even explode! If the cells are overcharged, quickly remove the charging lead and push the battery pack onto a hard surface – avoid actually touching it as it'll be extremely hot and likely to burn your hands. Cover it with a bucket or something similar and leave it alone for at least an hour to cool down. With any luck you may have caught it in time, but if the heat-shrink on the cells has melted and split there's a good chance the battery has been permanently damaged. It will then have to be thrown away and replaced.

Timer chargers – Timer chargers attempt to solve the overcharging problem by automatically switching off the charge after a set period. This is usually achieved using a clockwork timer attached to the resistor. Set the charge to ten minutes at a time and even if you become otherwise distracted you're much less likely to damage the cells. However, the total time taken to charge them will vary, so predicting when they're really ready for use may not be easy.

Temperature detect – Temperature detect chargers use a small probe that's applied onto or into the battery pack. This continually monitors the cell temperature and when a pre-set value is reached the charger automatically switches off the power. This works well as long as you always remember to insert the probe. If you don't, you'll have unintentionally reverted to the manual charge method and have become exposed to the same risk of blowing up the battery pack. The best

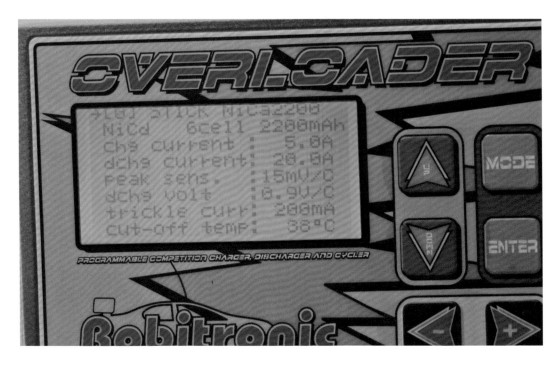

temperature detect chargers therefore combine the temperature probe with a timer, so that the power is cut after a certain time even if the pre-set temperature hasn't been reached.

Peak detect – The most popular and safest method of charging cells is with a peak detect charger. These continually monitor the battery voltage and shut the power off when the voltage starts to drop, which usually occurs when the cells are fully charged. The downside is that other events may cause a similar voltage drop to occur, causing the battery pack to 'false peak'. If this occurs while you're away chatting with friends, you may return to your pit table to find a partially charged pack of cells. False peaks are particularly common with cells that haven't been used for

some time, and can also be caused by poor connections.

Top-of-the-range peak detect chargers come with a whole host of extra features to control the charging process. The sensitivity of the peak detection can be adjusted to avoid false peaks, the charge rate can be changed to determine how quickly the energy should be transferred to the battery pack, and the total energy rating of the cells may even be recorded. Top drivers will use these features to their advantage during a race meeting. If they want slightly more duration from their cells, for example, they may drop the charge rate, sacrificing some punch from the cells for a slightly longer run time.

Battery technology is changing so rapidly, we strongly recommend that you follow the manufacturers' guidelines, making sure that your equipment is compatible to avoid inadvertent damage to the cells, your charger or yourself.

Discharging

After being used in the car a battery pack is likely to be very hot, so take care when removing it. If you've been racing round the garden at home the chances are that your car will have been driven until it stopped, so the battery pack is unlikely to have much usable energy left in it. If you've just competed in an organised race, however, the pack may not be fully flat and the remaining energy must be used up before it's recharged. This is the role of the discharger.

A suitable resistor or car bulb can be clipped

onto the battery pack to discharge the cells. Even better is to purchase a device specifically designed for this task. A commercial discharger will typically ensure the voltage of the cells isn't taken down too low, and may even discharge each cell individually. Some discharge boards are even fitted with cooling fans to reduce the temperature of the pack after use. When the pack is completely discharged it can be stored ready for reuse. It should not be reconnected to the charger until completely cool.

Buy three packs

It may take up to two hours to complete a full charge-use-discharge cycle, so if you intend to race at a local club it's a good idea to invest in three battery packs. A typical race meeting will consist of a practice session, four rounds of qualifying and a final, giving a total of six races. With three packs of cells you'll therefore be able to use each battery pack twice, while leaving plenty of time for each to cool down before being reconnected to the charger.

Final points

If you take good care of your battery packs, discharging them after each run, making sure they're cool before being recharged, and never overcharging them, they'll last for ages – 200 to 300 charges aren't uncommon. In fact the main reason radio control racers change their batteries isn't because they've stopped working, but because packs with even more capacity and even higher voltage have become available in the model shops. If the race duration hasn't been changed,

that means the car can be made to go even faster, which makes it even more exciting to drive.

Changing chassis settings

Weight distribution

Weight plays an important role on any racing car and a radio control car is no different. In competitions, it pays to run your car very close to the minimum weight allowed in your class. The

ABOVE A discharge board such as this one from Novak drains any remaining energy from each individual cell.

LEFT Three packs are enough for you to go racing without worrying about not getting charged in time.

ABOVE Don't be scared to make changes to your chassis settings.

heavier your car is, the more energy will be required to move it forward, make it stop, and get it to go round corners quickly. All that energy has to come from the motor and batteries in an electric car or from the engine and fuel in a nitro car, so by saving weight your car will either be faster or able to race for longer.

Before deciding to put your car through a major diet, though, get it weighed. Straight out of the box, the latest competition cars have been designed to be very close to the weight limits established by the sport's governing bodies. Take weight off and you can quickly end up having to add lumps of lead to make the car legal for racing.

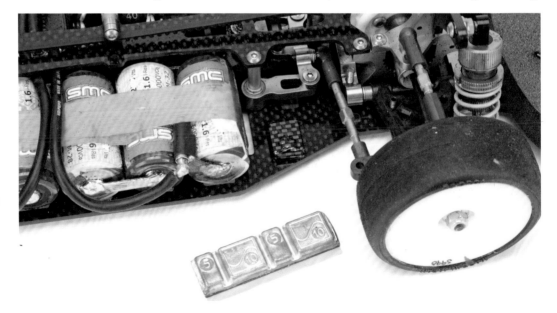

RIGHT Lead weight can be added to aid tuning or bring the overall weight of your car up to the minimum weight set out in the rules.

However, performance benefits can be obtained from reducing the weight of certain components. To identify where these parts are, it first helps to understand some of the science. On a model car, there are three types of weight to consider:

Sprung weight – The weight of the chassis and all the parts mounted on it are considered to be 'sprung weight'. These are the bits that bounce up and down on the springs of the car, such as the chassis itself, the shock towers, the radio equipment and the engine.

Unsprung weight – The moving suspension parts of the car that move up and down with the wheels, sit underneath the springs and have to react to all of the lumps and bumps on the track are considered to be 'unsprung weight'. Some suspension parts will have a proportion of both sprung and unsprung weight since they're attached to the chassis at one end (sprung) and the wheel at the other end (unsprung). The proportions of each can be calculated, but for an item such as a suspension arm 50 per cent of the weight will be unsprung (the average of the two ends). The heavier the suspension parts are, the

more inertia they will have in movement and a firmer shock absorber response will be needed to keep the wheels on the ground. Lighter wheels, inserts and tyres all help to reduce the unsprung weight and enable the shock absorbers to react more rapidly and accurately.

Rotating weight – All rotating mass is either sprung or unsprung. The armature in an electric motor, for example, is sprung, since it's held off the ground but also rotates. Similarly, the wheels are unsprung and they definitely rotate. In fact there are many rotating parts on a model car, such as the wheels, driveshafts, bearings, differentials, drivetrain and gears. Many of these are lightweight already and few gains can be made without affecting the reliability or handling of the car. Extra-lightweight plastic wheels, for example, may deform under heavy cornering, while thin drive-belts and gears can be much more susceptible to damage. The differentials and driveshafts may be prime candidates for weight reduction, though. Plastic composite driveshafts and aluminium differentials typically weigh substantially less than their steel equivalents.

ABOVE Parts of the chassis and suspension can be described as either sprung or unsprung. With this Hot Bodies Cyclone, using lightweight alloy driveshafts and wheel nuts helps to keep the unsprung weight to a minimum.

Now that we know the types of weight to consider, where is it worth trying to save a few grams? The answer comes in the ratio of sprung to unsprung weight. This is calculated by dividing the total sprung weight of the car by the total unsprung weight of all four wheels. A high ratio will give much improved handling on bumpy tracks, since the chassis won't be disturbed as much by the lighter wheels bouncing up and down. The inertia of the chassis will resist the movement of the tyres, keeping the rubber pressed firmly into contact with the bumpy track surface. And since the minimum weight limit for a model car is fixed by the rule book, the best way to increase this ratio is to reduce the unsprung weight and convert it into sprung weight. This can be achieved by fitting lightweight driveshafts, suspension arms, wheels and tyres. Small lead weights can then be added to the base of the chassis to increase the sprung weight. Another advantage of adding weight to the chassis is that you can decide exactly where it should go. It can be used to good effect to balance the car from left to right, perhaps to offset the extra mass of a motor mounted on one side of the car.

Of course, things get even more interesting when the car is racing round the track, since forces now act on all of that weight and this affects the handling of the car.

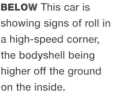

BELOW This car is showing signs of roll in a high-speed corner, the bodyshell being higher off the ground on the inside.

Weight transfer

When a model touring car accelerates it's subjected to an inertia force, which acts in the opposite direction to the force pushing the car forward. When accelerating hard in a real car you can feel the effect of this force as it pushes you back into the seat. The inertia force acts on the car's centre of gravity, a point that sits some distance above the chassis. The effect of the accelerating force pushing the car forward at ground level, and the inertia force pushing backwards at the higher centre of gravity, is to lift the front of the car. This is most noticeable on a vehicle with a very high centre of gravity, such as a motorcycle, where rapid acceleration will result in a wheelie. Under acceleration, weight is therefore reduced at the front of the car and increased by the same amount at the rear. This doesn't usually help to improve traction, since the increased vertical force pushing down on the car can distort the tyres and reduce the amount of grip they provide.

Weight transfer works in the opposite direction under braking. This time the inertia force reduces the vertical force on the rear tyres and increases the vertical force on the front tyres. In a full-size car, the inertia force under heavy braking throws you forward onto the seat belt.

Lateral weight transfer occurs when the car

goes round corners and is called 'roll'. This time, weight is removed from the inside tyres and added to the outside tyres. No matter how the car is set up, if the inside tyre transfers as much weight as it had on it when the car was stationary then that wheel will lift up off the track. Since driving a three-wheeler isn't a great way to win races, a set-up change will then be needed to

increase the roll stiffness on the car and get all four wheels back onto the track. During cornering, the grip on the inside tyre increases due to the reduced vertical force, but not as much as the outside tyre loses grip due to the weight transfer. The car will therefore corner faster if the lateral weight transfer can be minimised, something that can be achieved by adjusting the suspension.

ABOVE Weight transfer occurs when accelerating and decelerating/braking. Weight moves forward as you come off the throttle or brake, whereas when you apply the throttle the weight will move rearwards.

LEFT Roll is lateral weight transfer. As the chassis goes round a left-hand corner the weight will roll towards the right-hand side and vice versa.

Calculating weight distribution

Corner weight is the weight supported at each tyre contact patch. Adding up all four corner weights gives the total weight of the car. The values are likely to differ from front to rear as the overall weight distribution is rarely an exact 50:50 split. The weights are also likely to differ from side to side since it's usually not possible to mount all of the components in a car in a completely symmetrical manner.

Ideally you need two sets of digital scales to measure the corner weight, together with a set of

blocks that can be placed under the other end of the car to keep the chassis level while weighing. Always bounce the car slightly before taking a reading and always weigh the car in a ready-to-race state, with the fuel on board if it's a nitro car, or with the battery in place if racing in the electric class. After taking readings from each corner, the weight distribution can be calculated. For balanced handling the front to rear ratio on both the left-hand and right-hand sides should match the front-to-rear weight distribution of the whole car.

Staying legal

The differing weights of wheel/tyre/insert combinations are one of the main causes of disqualification at Championship events. Drivers change tyres without reweighing their cars and then fail post-race scrutineering due to the new combination dropping their car below the legal limit. If you change tyres, always play it safe and get the car reweighed before you go out to race.

Setting the suspension

Compromise is the key when it comes to perfecting the suspension set-up of a radio control car. The possibilities for adjustment are vast and it can take many runs to get close to the ultimate combination of settings for a particular track. If you

discover the handling isn't quite to your liking, which setting should you change? The springs, oil, pistons, limiters, mounting points, ride height, or anti-roll bars? At least with a model car there's one compromise you don't have to make: there's no need to be concerned about the comfort of the ride when there's no driver on board!

By itself the suspension doesn't generate grip. That's the job of the tyres. The suspension is there to ensure all four wheels remain firmly on the ground at all times, keeping the contact patch of the tyres as large as possible. During braking and cornering, weight transfer changes the attitude of the car, making the suspension move relative to the chassis. Under braking the weight transfers forwards, making the chassis load up the front springs. This compresses the springs and forces the car into a nose-down attitude, often referred to as positive pitch. Under cornering the weight transfers sideways, compressing the springs on the outside of the car so that it leans or rolls outwards. The suspension links also pivot about their chassis mounting points and their outboard mountings on the suspension arms. These movements cause the wheels to adopt different angles to the static settings, which changes the size and shape of the tyre contact patch.

This is where the compromises begin. A suspension design that keeps the wheels upright under the pitch caused by braking will cause large angular changes to the wheels during the roll induced by cornering, resulting in a smaller tyre contact patch. If the suspension is optimised for pitch changes, then it requires a method of limiting roll in order to limit the changes in wheel angle. If the suspension is optimised for roll, then the car

needs a means of controlling the pitch. Not surprisingly, RC car designers therefore spend many hours trying to design a suspension geometry that provides the best compromise. They also provide plenty of adjustability so that every driver can make their own desired changes from track to track.

All manner of adjustments can be made to the shock absorbers, such as changing the springs, damper oil, pistons, and packers.

Changing the damper oil affects the 'static' damping, which is what you feel when you move the piston rod in and out. Generally, static

RIGHT This range of shock pistons shows the one with the largest holes on the left, through to the one with the smallest holes on the right. The piston on the far right will have more 'pack' than the one on the far left.

damping affects the handling of the car as it turns into and exits a corner, and as the car travels over gentle bumps. When the bumps get really severe the piston has to react quickly, and that depends on how quickly the oil can pass through the holes. The ability to react is called 'pack'.

Pack is therefore the rate at which the piston can react to any quick, sharp movement from the suspension. Less, or smaller, holes slow down the piston's reaction and the damper has more pack. Larger or more holes speed up the piston's ability to react and it consequently has less pack. Pack affects the car as it lands from large jumps, or travels through a series of medium to large jumps.

There's a limit to how fast a piston can move through shock oil. The size of the piston's holes and the thickness of the oil determine the piston's 'maximum speed limit' as it moves through the oil. If the shock was compressed faster than the piston's speed limit, the resistance of the shock would be greatly increased – it might even 'lock up'. Pistons with large holes have a higher speed limit than pistons with small holes. Therefore if you install large-hole pistons in your shocks your

suspension will be better able to cope with bumps and jumps taken at high speed. Smaller-hole pistons improve cornering (because the shocks will limit chassis roll and brake dive) and jumping (because the suspension will be less compressed by the face of the jump).

Make the springs too stiff and the car will become very nervous, likely to fly off into the undergrowth at every opportunity. It won't put the power down well, is more likely to slide round the corners rather than grip, and may skid if the brakes are slammed on hard. No fun, and slow too! A car that's too soft will be sluggish to respond when entering corners, and will roll and pitch excessively under cornering and braking. It may also scrape the ground under certain conditions such as heavy braking. Imbalances in front and rear spring stiffness can cause handling and cornering imbalances. Go too stiff at the front and the car will understeer too much, while a car that's too stiff at the rear will oversteer, possibly kicking the rear end out into a slide.

On a track offering reasonable traction you can often gain insight into how effective your

BELOW Colour-coded springs clearly indicate the different rates so that there's no confusion when it comes to changing them.

suspension settings have been by examining the surface of your tyres after a race. If the outside edges show visible signs of doing more work than the rest of the tyre (such as scuff marks, or pitting on the rubber), then the suspension may be allowing too much positive camber to be generated during cornering, or there may be too little static negative camber. To reduce the amount of roll that occurs, increase the stiffness of the springs or fit a thicker anti-roll bar. Alternatively, increase the static negative camber to spread the load more evenly when cornering. Examining the tyres again after the next race will tell you how successful your adjustments have been.

Gearing it right

The gearing provides your car with its mix of top speed, acceleration and duration. Every revolution of the engine or motor will result in the car moving forward and the distance it travels is determined by the gearing. Because of this, the gearing is typically expressed in millimetres per rev (MMPR). Such a measure enables direct comparisons to be made between different makes of car, even when they're running on different profile tyres, or are using different pinion and spur gears.

The MMPR on which your car should be geared depends on a whole host of factors, not least the number of minutes you're racing for and the size of the circuit. A high MMPR will typically give a greater top speed, but at the expense of acceleration and duration. Conversely, a low MMPR will let the engine rev, giving good acceleration and improved duration but a slower top speed. With a nitro-powered car the gearing is a major factor in determining the time between pit stops; the fewer stops you need to make for fuel, the more time you'll spend on the race track.

To calculate the MMPR, a simple mathematical formula is used that takes into account the size of the tyres, the number of teeth on the spur gear and pinion and, for a four-wheel-drive car, the internal gearbox ratio, sometimes referred to as the 'final drive ratio'. You'll need to check the instructions included in the kit to find the value for your car. The formula to calculate the MMPR is:

$$\text{Tyre diameter (mm)} \times \frac{\pi}{\left(\dfrac{\text{number of spur teeth}}{\text{number of pinion teeth}}\right) \times \text{drive ratio}}$$

As an example, consider an electric-powered touring car running on low profile tyres. Using a

Vernier gauge, we find the tyres are 58mm in diameter, so multiplying these by π (3.1416) gives us the circumference of the tyre. We then divide that by the number of teeth on the spur gear and multiply the result by the number of teeth on the pinion. Finally we divide the result by the final drive ratio, as documented in the instruction booklet. For this example, let's assume that the spur gear size is 72-teeth and we would use a 32-tooth pinion on a large track, and a 22-tooth pinion on a smaller one. We are going to base the calculations on the assumption that the figure for π is 3.1416 and the internal ratio, or IR, is 2.5:1. So the MMPR for a couple of very different circuits may be:

Large outdoor tarmac track:
$$\text{MMPR} = 58 \times \frac{3.1416}{\left(\dfrac{72}{32}\right) \times 2.5} = 32.4$$

Small indoor track:
$$\text{MMPR} = 58 \times \frac{3.1416}{\left(\dfrac{72}{22}\right) \times 2.5} = 22.3$$

ABOVE Which pinion should you use? Consulting the instruction manual is a good starting point.

BELOW You must achieve a balance of top speed on the straight and acceleration out of the corners.

ABOVE Your gearing options are much greater with a two-speed gearbox set-up on a nitro-powered on-road chassis.

ABOVE RIGHT Over-gearing on an electric-powered model will result in increased operating temperatures.

RIGHT Make up a simple gear ratio chart like this one so that you can make accurate changes trackside. The large numbers across the chart refer to the size of spur gear, with the pinion size running vertically.

On the large tarmac circuit the 32-tooth pinion provides a high MMPR, so the car will move further for each rev of the motor. This gives it a high top speed, but at the expense of acceleration. This is fine on wide flowing circuits where the speed of the car can be maintained through the corners, but throw in a few hairpins and coming down a couple of teeth on the pinion can provide a better compromise. Indoors on the small circuit, the straights are much shorter and the corners are tighter. Acceleration therefore becomes more important than top speed, making it better to run a much smaller pinion.

Unless you're an ace at mathematics you'll need to take a calculator with you to work out the MMPR. However, most drivers tend to use the same car, the same diameter tyres and the same spur gear throughout a race meeting. It's therefore a pretty easy task to calculate the MMPR for each of the pinions you happen to have in your toolbox. Record these in a table and it'll be easy to see the effect of moving up or down a tooth. Record next to this the circuits on which a particular pinion was run and you'll quickly build up a very useful gearing guide. You can also check the internet or model car magazines to get a guide to the gearing used by some of the top drivers.

The MMPR calculations get even more interesting for a nitro-powered car fitted with a multi-speed gearbox. On this you need to calculate the MMPR for each available spur/pinion combination, and then decide the engine revs at which the gearbox should change from one pinion to the other. Get this right and you can obtain the perfect compromise between acceleration and top speed for any circuit. A two- or three-tooth gap between the gears often works best. With more

IR 2.31:1	Team Losi XX-4		
	78	82	84
14	12.87	13.53	13.86
15	12.01	12.63	12.94
16	11.26	11.84	12.13
17	10.60	11.14	11.41
18	10.01	10.52	10.78
19	9.48	9.97	10.21
20	9.01	9.47	9.70
21	8.58	9.02	9.24
22	8.19	8.61	8.82
23	7.83	8.24	8.44
24	7.51	7.89	8.09
25	7.21	7.58	7.76
26	6.93	7.29	7.46
27	6.67	7.02	7.19

IR 2.60:1	Team Associated RC10B4		
	78	81	84
14	11.93	12.39	12.85
15	11.27	11.70	12.13
16	10.67	11.08	11.49
17	10.14	10.53	10.92
18	9.66	10.03	10.40
19	9.22	9.57	9.93
20	8.82	9.16	9.50
21	8.45	8.78	9.10
22	8.11	8.42	8.74
23	7.80	8.10	8.40
24	7.51	7.80	8.09
25	7.24	7.52	7.80
26	6.99	7.26	7.53
27	6.76	7.02	7.28

than a four-tooth gap the gears may be susceptible to damage.

With an electric-powered car your choice of motor will influence the required gearing. A stock motor will not rev as highly as a modified motor, for example, so it needs to be geared on a higher MMPR in order for the car to reach the same top speed. If you have any doubts at all about the gearing on which to run a particular motor, always play on the safe side and run a small pinion. Under-gearing a motor simply allows it to rev more and will do the motor much less harm than over-gearing it. Running too large a pinion can put the motor under a lot of strain, resulting in a high current draw. With a brushed motor, the commutator will get scored or marked, brushes will start to discolour and the motor-can may lose some magnetism. Such changes will eventually happen to a correctly geared motor too, but it'll take many more races before the effects begin to show.

With an off-road model the gearing can be simplified, as there's no need to measure the size of the tyres and this means you can make up a simple gear ratio chart, as shown.

Bodyshells

There are three great things about bodyshells: they can be changed, there's plenty of choice, and you can paint them any colour you like. Less appealing is the fact that preparing a good-looking paint scheme often takes a considerable amount of time; time you might not want to spend when you're eager to get your new car onto the racetrack. But as well as making your vehicle look the part, bodyshells have two other important

roles to play: they help prevent your car being damaged and they help it to handle properly. Thin and flimsy pieces of plastic they may be, but you'll be amazed at the amount of punishment they can take, and it takes a very serious accident indeed to actually destroy one.

Aerodynamics play a significant role in the handling of full-size racing cars, and they also affect the handling of radio control cars. If you don't believe this, simply remove the rear wing from your RC touring car and then attempt to drive it. Suddenly it becomes very loose on the rear in high-speed turns and is much less stable on the track. This is because the curves on the bodyshell and the rear wing create downforce, a pressure that helps push the car down onto the circuit. This gives you better control in the corners, but less speed on the straights because of increased aerodynamic drag.

Aerodynamics are one of the key areas of focus for full-size racing teams, who spend a lot of time performing wind tunnel tests in an attempt to

ABOVE There's a massive range of bodyshells available that all have different aerodynamic properties.

BELOW Some bodyshell designs will have better high- or low-speed handling.

ABOVE Craig Drescher looks to tweak the mounting of his bodyshell.

generate more downforce without increasing drag. While the aerodynamics on model cars aren't as sensitive as those on a full-size race car, the body shape can still significantly change the way the car handles. Unless you enjoy 'doing doughnuts', all touring car shells must be run with a rear wing, ideally one that fits the maximum dimensions allowed in the rule book. To provide maximum benefit this is usually mounted as high and as far back as the rules allow. On large, high traction circuits, however, the wing can be lowered or cut-down to reduce drag and slightly increase the top speed of the car.

One of the advantages of lightweight bodyshells is that they can be quickly changed. While altering the aerodynamics in this way provides another way to tune your car for a particular track, it also allows you to change the appearance of the car to suit your own personal taste, or to make it eligible for an alternative race series. In the on-road classes, sports car shells tend to sit much lower than a touring car bodyshell, so in theory they should generate less

drag and result in a quicker car. In practice there's usually a price to pay in reduced downforce so that the time gained on the straight is then lost in the corners. In particular the absence of a steeply-raked front results in less front-end downforce, which tends to promote understeer. Rally car shells are mounted much higher on the car to allow for increased suspension travel and normally come complete with a very large rear wing. Racing on loose surfaces downforce is more important than drag, so this is what the rally bodyshell strives to achieve.

Wheels and tyres

Top RC racing drivers put a lot of emphasis on their choice of tyres, inserts and wheels. Some even claim that these can contribute as much as 70 per cent to the car's handling. One thing's for sure – getting the tyre, insert and wheel combination right is crucial to good handling and a quick car.

Choosing the right tyres is determined by where you intend to race. Some tyres work better on certain tracks than others and the only way to find out which is going to suit your track and therefore give you the most grip is by asking someone. Once you've found out what tyres the local drivers are using you'll have to try them with different inserts. A thin soft insert which leaves an air gap between it and the tyre will allow the rubber to heat up to its optimum operating temperature faster and is therefore ideal in cooler conditions, whereas a thick insert that fills the tyre will stop it heating up so fast and may be a better choice when it's warmer.

Tyre choice is also determined by track temperature. If the weather's hot and the tarmac warm then a harder rubber will be preferable. The

RIGHT They may all look the same but there are massive differences between one tyre and another.

FAR RIGHT Some manufacturers indicate the 'rating' of their tyre by moulding it into the sidewall.

opposite is true if you're racing in cooler conditions. The basic rule of thumb is if the tyres are squealing when going around corners they're probably too soft and may be overheating. Check the wear rate, and if they're showing signs of graining change to a harder tyre. These days tyres are usually rated for different temperatures and guidance is often given on the packaging.

Wheels can also make a difference to a car's handling. Stiffer wheels will make the tyres and suspension work harder, whereas a more compliant, softer wheel will absorb some of the bumps and help to smooth the car out.

Drifting

While most radio control on-road racers still spend their money trying to prevent their cars from sliding, an altogether different trend has emerged from Japan. It turns out that despite the quest for more traction and faster lap times it's actually a whole lot more fun to drive RC cars completely sideways!

Like many of the best ideas, the concept originated in full-size racing. Drifting began as a secret 'underground' event, sliding round treacherous mountainous roads in Japan. But the spectacle soon moved to the racetrack, where thousands of fans now attend D1 Drift Grand Prix events and many websites and magazines actively promote the sport. The radio control version mirrors reality in that any advantage comes not from outright horsepower, but from smooth style and control. The more skilful the driver, the longer they can hold the car in a drift and the more sideways they're able to corner. Dedicated radio control drift meetings are now being held, many of them copying the full-size practice of using a

panel of judges to assess the sideways prowess and style of the drivers.

Special tyres are the necessity for going sideways. These are typically narrow and made from a very hard rubber compound. A key advantage of having so little grip available is that you then don't need lots of power to push the car sideways. A stock motor usually proves perfectly adequate for drifting, and crucially it also provides the controllability needed to smoothly slide round the corners.

But by far the most important aspect of drifting is to create the right look. Iconic, 1980s-style Japanese coupés are all the rage – retro designs like the Mazda RX-7, Nissan 180SX, Toyota Trueno or Nissan Skyline. With long bonnets and tiny rear wings, these shells already look very different to your average competition saloon, but to give them that special street appearance you also need to add plenty of 'bling', with chrome wheels, fake brake discs and custom tailpipes. Add a trick custom paint scheme and a few neon light strips and you'll be ready to drift in true fast and furious style!

ABOVE LEFT Not only are the tyres and moulded inserts available in different compounds but the wheels can be purchased in different stiffnesses.

ABOVE Drifting is a growing aspect of RC, paralleling the success of its full-size motor sport counterpart. *(CML Distribution)*

BELOW You can really go to town on a drift car, with flashy paint schemes, extreme wheels and lights.

Driving the car

The best part of ownership	110
Choosing radio gear	110
Driving techniques	116
Mastering jumps	120
Problem solving	124

The best part of ownership

Every RC owner has a transmitter and they come in all shapes and sizes, ranging in price from around £10 to more than £300. You don't have to have a top-of-the-range item to be successful but the additional functionality of the higher-end transmitters can certainly make your life easier as a model car driver. Most of us start with a simple two-channel radio with just a few features such as a battery LED, servo reverse and adjustable trims.

ABOVE Racing further develops your RC driving skills.
(www.oople.com}

The majority of basic radios are stick design, although with the increase in the number of RTR kits from overseas manufacturers many new RC drivers are learning with steerwheel units. Either way, it's likely that you'll continue to use whatever type of unit you started with, as only the very best drivers are able to switch from one format to the other. But whatever your preference, there's a radio out there that can offer more features and actually increase your enjoyment. In this chapter we'll look at the most popular ranges of radio on the market, their functions, and how they can improve your driving.

Choosing radio gear

The term 'radio gear' is often used as a generalisation to refer to all the radio control equipment that's used to make your model car respond the way you want it to. This includes the transmitter that's used to input and then send the signals to control the car, the receiver that picks up the signals, and the servos used for the steering and throttle.

In many ways choosing what transmitter and radio gear to use is more important than choosing what car to drive. The transmitter, or radio as it's often called, is what connects you to your RC model, so it has to be comfortable to hold, be responsive, have all the functions you're likely to need and, above all, be reliable in operation. Many transmitters today offer a multi-model memory that enables you to program and save different settings separately. This means you only have to use one transmitter and can swap between many different models without having to re-trim or re-adjust any settings.

Good radio gear isn't cheap, but it will last a long time and can be transferred from one car to another, so choosing the right equipment from the start is very important. View it as a long-term investment that, if looked after, should give you years of service.

As with most things in life, when it comes to radio gear you usually get what you pay for. Generally the more expensive the radio gear the more functions it will perform and the faster it will respond. What you buy is ultimately decided by what model you intend to use it in. There's no point spending a fortune on the latest high-speed servos and digital transmitter if you only intend to run your car around the back garden or in the park. There's plenty of good quality low-cost radio gear around that'll be up to that task. But if you're serious about racing you might want to spend a bit more and go for faster servos and a transmitter with more

functions, such as model memories and digital trims and lap timers.

Wheel versus stick

Stick transmitters have always been the preferred choice in the UK, but with more and more young drivers being brought up on a diet of RTR cars supplied with steerwheel radios the market for top-end wheel sets has increased.

Steerwheel, pistol-grip or wheel-and-trigger transmitters, as they're variously known, are widely used for controlling RC cars around the world. In fact the UK is really the odd man out when it comes to

ABOVE 'Radio gear' refers to items such as servos, receivers and receiver packs.

FAR LEFT The Esprit III from KO Propo is the most modern of the stick forms of transmitter.

LEFT JR Propo's R-1 steerwheel radio complete with large LCD display.

comes to our love of the stick transmitter, the popularity of which dates back to the early days of RC cars when enthusiasts who'd been flying model planes brought their radio gear, including their stick transmitters, over to use with cars.

Not only does controlling an RC car using a wheel transmitter seem to make sense, it also has certain advantages. When driving using your thumbs on a stick transmitter it can be quite difficult to simultaneously use your other fingers to operate other functions on the radio, such as timers and trims. With a steerwheel radio these problems are eliminated. The throttle and brake are operated using your index finger, which is a lot stronger and faster than your thumb, and it leaves your thumb on that hand free to operate other functions on the radio. It's for this reason that most wheel transmitters have their trim switches located around the throttle and wheel area so that they can be operated with the free thumb. Also the steering input is made using all the fingers and thumb on your other hand, which means you have more strength and potentially faster reaction time.

This sounds great, but if you've been driving an RC car for a long time using a stick radio it's very difficult indeed to suddenly start driving using a wheel. Though some drivers have proved that it's possible to make the switch, it takes a lot of practice and it's pretty certain that if you're a competitive racer you're not going to be as quick with a wheel straight away. Some may feel that the advantages of a wheel radio are worth the sacrifice, but most will probably stick to what they know.

Servos

We already know that the transmitter's important, as it's what connects the driver to the car, and a good quality receiver is required to pick up the signals and interpret what the driver wants the car to do. But another piece of radio gear that's just as important is the servo. This plays an important role in translating the signal inputs from the receiver into a rotary movement that, by the clever use of linkages, results in either the steering movement of the wheels or the opening/closing of the engine carburettor.

Most low-cost radio packages will come complete with either one or two basic servos, which will be fine to begin with; but there's a huge array of higher quality after-market servos available that, even if you don't intend to race and compete, will make controlling your RC car much easier and more enjoyable.

Although they may look the same, the differences between basic and high-end servos are numerous. Firstly, the shaft output will be supported on a ball race bearing as opposed to a metal bush, which will make it more durable. In addition metal gears are often found in many high-end servos, which again make the servo more resilient to impact damage and are recommended for steering duties.

Speed and torque are two figures that are very important when choosing an appropriate servo for your application. Most manufacturers will quote speed in terms of the time (seconds) it takes for the servo to complete a given angle of rotation

RIGHT Servos can range from under £10 to around £130 for top-of-the-range examples. This selection comes from Sanwa.

(degrees). Generally, a faster servo (lower time per given angle) will feel more responsive in a car, but unless it has enough torque to overcome the load being placed by the wheels or throttle linkage this figure may be misleading.

Thus torque – or the load that the servo can move – is equally important. As a rule larger and heavier cars will require more torque to move the steering, and steering servos are likely to be under more load than a throttle servo. It's perfectly acceptable to mix different servos from the same manufacturer with your receiver and, in most cases, even use a different make of servo and receiver; but in some cases, especially with the top-end servos, some of the digital programming features or the highest response settings can only be achieved when using a servo and receiver pairing from the same manufacturer.

When you first drive your car with faster or higher torque servos, the difference is amazing. The response will occur much sooner than you anticipate, and the additional control that you have over the standard servos will enable you to be more accurate with your throttle control (especially useful when trying to master the art of jumping) and your steering, thus enabling you to lap quicker and more consistently.

Digital servos

Without doubt, digital or FET servos have provided a breakthrough in servo drive technology in recent years. Traditional analogue servos process the receiver signal via a logic chip and timing components but digital servos use an onboard microprocessor which can be programmed to alter some of the operating parameters and characteristics, thus offering increased control for experienced drivers.

Any servo operates by driving a tiny electric motor within the servo to turn the gears and output shaft. The difference between analogue and digital technology is that modern digital servos pulse the motor supply 300 times per second, as opposed to the analogue control circuitry which pulses the motor only 50 times per second. This has two effects. Firstly, it provides a much quicker response to any given input signal; and secondly, it provides far greater control over small input changes and enables far greater holding torque.

The downside of all this technical trickery is that a digital servo tends to consume more power than its analogue counterpart. Thus in some electric-powered classes many racers continue to opt for an analogue steering servo because it doesn't drain as much power from the main battery which is used to drive the motor and ESC. However, with

battery technology providing more and more capacity in any given cell size this is becoming less of an issue.

It may seem a strange upgrade initially, since it doesn't directly offer any improvements in power or car speed, but choosing the correct servo for your application will result in faster lap times and improved enjoyment through enhanced control.

2.4GHz equipment

The most recent advance in radio technology has seen a boom in the development of 2.4GHz equipment – a notable jump in frequency from the 27MHz and 40MHz that most kits come with. These new radio systems eliminate the need to follow the usual track protocol of selecting an open frequency using a pegboard before turning on. Instead, you simply switch on your transmitter and it then automatically scans all of the available frequencies and locks onto one that's available. When you switch your transmitter off, the frequency will automatically be released for someone else to use. In fact, with a system like this the days of suffering radio interference caused by another driver switching on a transmitter using the same frequency will be over – and if everyone used it the pegboard would become redundant too!

Such equipment became a reality at the end of 2005, when approval was granted to use radio control systems based on 'Direct Sequencing Spread Spectrum' technology, as pioneered by the Spektrum system. This technical marvel can search all 79 allocated frequencies in the 2.4GHz band and

LEFT Spread-Spectrum equipment such as this shows how the 2.4GHz frequency is becoming more widespread in RC use, and not just for wireless applications at home and in the office.

Radio terms

Anti-lock brakes – This is a feature often used by nitro racers where the servo position is pulsed during operation rather than being held in a fixed position, which in turn prevents the car's wheels from locking up. It can also be referred to as an 'anti-lock braking system' or ABS.

End-point adjustment – 'EPA' is an invaluable feature that allows you to ensure the servos move to their maximum position without straining, which can cause damage. When used on the steering it can be used to ensure that the car's turning circle is set to be the same arc regardless of whether it's turning left or right. On a nitro car the EPA can be used to precisely adjust the servo travel for the throttle and brake, all without having to change the servo's neutral point. Over-throwing a servo (where the servo tries to force the linkage to move further than is mechanically enabled) will cause damage to the servo's motor in the long term. Therefore EPA enables you to tune the servo throw to the mechanical package limitations of the linkage.

Exponential – Exponential affects the amount of servo movement obtained from any given transmitter movement. For a linear set up, the servo movement directly corresponds to the transmitter movement – *ie* move the transmitter 25 per cent

ABOVE Getting to know your radio and what it can do.

RIGHT Whether your radio utilises 27 or 40MHz, you'll need crystals.

through the travel and you obtain 25 per cent of the available servo travel. Negative exponential would result in less initial servo travel for the same amount of transmitter input – *ie* 25 per cent transmitter input would result in 15 per cent of servo movement. This has the effect of taming the initial servo response and making the car feel easier to drive. It's normally used on the steering since it allows the initial movement of the control to be 'softened', making the steering less responsive when the transmitter control is moved a tiny amount. Some nitro drivers add a little expo to their throttle if the conditions are slippery, as it follows the same logic as when used on the steering.

Frequency – As standard, a transmitter operates on a set range of frequencies. Most RTR models are supplied with 27MHz equipment, whilst the 40MHz range was more commonly found in uprated radio sets offering a greater spread. Nowadays the 2.4GHz frequency is becoming more popular with up to 79 free channels and automatic selection. RC cars can operate on all three of these frequency ranges, whereas aircraft are limited to 35MHz and 2.4GHz. It's important to understand that the operating frequencies used for RC cars are allocated by national governments and under strict legal control. Penalties for misuse of frequencies are often severe, as effectively you're then transmitting a signal on an unauthorised frequency – much like a 'pirate' radio station would. Confiscation of equipment and a hefty financial penalty will result if a successful prosecution is bought against unlawful operation.

Model memory – If you race more than one class of car or have many models, then a transmitter with a model memory is beneficial. This allows different settings to be programmed and stored for different cars. When the transmitter is switched on, simply selecting the appropriate car will restore the transmitter settings previously assigned to that model.

Servo reverse – Since there's no standard way for servos to be fitted into a car, on some models they may operate in the opposite direction to others. However, if the transmitter control is moved to the right and the car then turns left it will prove rather tricky to drive. With servo reverse, the commands can be reversed on the transmitter without having to adjust the fitting of the servos.

Steering rate – If your car is turning too sharply (in the corners, for example), dialling in less movement of the steering servo may provide a temporary cure. You reduce the movement or rate on some transmitters by operating a small dial. The normal range of adjustment can be from full down to as little as 20 per cent.

LEFT Even the most basic of transmitters will have a servo reversing option.

then lock onto one that's free. Interference protection is also improved through the use of a unique identification key. When the receiver detects an incoming signal, it first checks the identification key to confirm that the signal came from your transmitter. If it didn't, the signal is simply ignored. Another bonus is that the 2.4GHz band is a long way away from other frequencies generated inside the car, such as those caused by arcing motors, vibrating metal parts and speed controls. These frequencies typically occur at less than 300MHz and have to be suppressed when using a conventional radio system by fitting appropriate capacitors and diodes.

And if that still doesn't sound good enough, the 2.4GHz units are the fastest responding radio systems around, the transmitter uses a lot less power than normal, and the very short receiver aerial can actually remain *inside* the bodyshell of the car. What's more, the receiver is even capable of transmitting signals from the car back to the pit area, opening up a wealth of future possibilities for on-board telemetry systems. It's no wonder that many drivers have started converting their radio systems to the 2.4GHz operating band!

Driving techniques

Whether you wish to reach the top step of the podium or just fancy increasing your enjoyment of the hobby, learning to drive your RC model as well as you can is vital. Honing your skills by practising will help you get the best from your equipment and make your lap times faster. Having all the best gear will be wasted if you crash on every jump and miss every other apex. You may be thinking that this won't be a problem as you only want to use your truck down the local park, but even then there'll be circumstances where you may have to avoid benches, goalposts or other park users.

Anyone can drive an RC car around a large open area like a field or empty car park, but that way you'll never benefit from the investment you've made in the chassis. So first of all you need to set up a series of obstacles to drive around. This will give you a set of specific points where you'll need to slow down and brake, turn in and accelerate away from. By developing your skills on this kind of basic layout, when you come to putting your car on a track you'll have experience that will prove invaluable.

BELOW Keeping your model on its wheels and not crashing is the secret to being a winner on the track. *(Thorsten Gora)*

Don't get too carried away with the throttle at first. Modern RC cars are extremely fast so you just need to make small movements on the throttle and concentrate on the steering. One good tip to remember is that there's no need to constantly adjust the steering – too many novices make adjustments to the steering and this actually makes it harder for you to grasp the skills. Another piece of advice is that you'll find steering becomes notably harder when the car comes towards you, since to move it to the right you must turn the steering to the left. After a while, however, this will become second nature and you won't need to consciously think about the movements needed on the transmitter controls.

One man band

It's definitely better to be on your own when practising, as having anyone watching will only put you off. You'll need to find a suitable open area where there's plenty of space for you to lay out some cones, such as a car park when the shops are shut, or an empty field. Be aware of the implications of what you're doing – nitro cars are noisy, so it isn't acceptable to practise close to houses on a weekend, for instance. Although an

ABOVE Landing this heavily and nose first is not the fastest way to jump. *(Thorsten Gora)*

LEFT Practising on your own is the best way to learn, as you can use the whole track without fear of getting in another racer's way.

ABOVE After getting in some quality practice, the next step is your local club and the chance to put that practice to the test.

FAR RIGHT This diagram depicts the three aspects of a corner, indicated by the yellow rectangles: these are the turn-in point, the apex, and a clipping point for the exit. This is an ideal scenario based on a track where the grip levels are consistent throughout the width and duration of the corner.

empty field may therefore seem ideal, make sure that the owner is happy for you to use it and that there are no animals nearby that could be alarmed.

The next thing to do is choose a point from which you can watch the car and clearly see the cones – remember that if you're going to a track you won't be able to follow the car round, so driving it from a distance is a vital skill you'll need to learn. A raised area such as a bench or low wall may give you a better view.

Once you've selected a suitable vantage point you can begin to drive round. Starting slowly at first, you should be able to negotiate the cones to create a lap, gradually increasing your speed while trying not to make mistakes. Try not to simply go as fast as possible, as crashing will cost you more time in a race situation than going flat out down the straight. The key is to get in plenty of practice, familiarising yourself with the controls and the handling.

The next step

The urge will be to get down to your local track as quickly as possible after just a few practice sessions, but it's the time spent on your own that will pay dividends when you go to an unfamiliar venue. There are many purpose-built tracks around the country where you can put your skills to the test, but you may wish to carry out some homework before you attend your first race day. Get down to a club race to see how the meeting runs, to find out the timetable and to see if there's anything that you may need. Many clubs will have different classes competing on the same day, so you can find out which category you can race in and what other requirements the club may have. For example, until now you may only have needed one set of crystals but you may have to invest in a

second set. Also, you may need a source of power to recharge your batteries or receiver pack, so most racers bring a 12V battery with them. A visit also provides an opportunity to talk to the organisers and other racers, as well as to walk around the track and familiarise yourself with the set-up. This homework will give you more confidence when you attend next time, as you'll have a better understanding of the meeting's format.

You need to turn up with everything that you need for a day's racing, and in plenty of time to sort your stuff out and get ready for practice. Always walk the track before you drive round it – this allows you to closely inspect the track and assess your lines so that you have a good idea of where you're going to go. It will also ensure that you're aware of bumps and jumps that may not be visible from the rostrum. When you do get onto the track don't expect to be the fastest car – there are bound to be some very good club drivers blasting past you, as they know their cars and track very well. Instead, learn from them and work out why they can go through a particular section faster, and try to understand the racing lines that they're using. Your first few laps should be negotiated slowly so that you can learn the layout. Then gradually increase your speed, remembering to keep it smooth and tidy. With unfamiliar tracks, or a new car, remembering the basics rather than trying to run as fast as possible will often result in quicker improvements to your lap times. Remember, you have to walk before you can run.

Slow in, fast out

The quickest way round the corners is the one that maintains the highest corner speed and minimum amount of steering input. This will keep the car going in the straightest possible line and therefore keeps the speed high. Basically, the corners should be

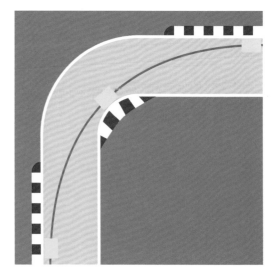

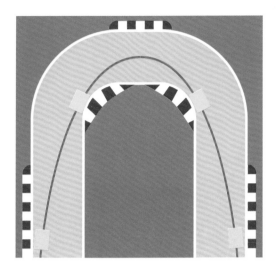

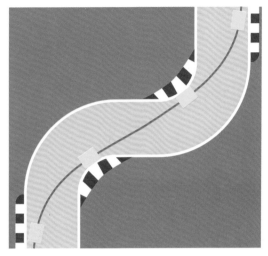

FAR LEFT With a hairpin, there's a chance that you might not use the whole of the track but the same principle applies, of turn-in, double apex and exit points. Note that it may be necessary to tighten the corner in the middle rather than maintain a constant radius.

LEFT This diagram demonstrates the perfect line through a multiple corner section such as a chicane, where you try to make the series of corners as straight as possible so that you retain the highest corner speed.

made into a continuous flow without any sharp movements. The best drivers in the world achieve their status not only due to their ability but also because they're able to read the track quickly and react to other drivers. When coming up to slower cars, instead of making last minute direction changes they work out whether they should hold back for a corner or take an alternative line to pass them. Time lost being placed back on the track by a marshal can very rarely be made up by driving quickly.

Slow down

Using the brakes in the correct manner will help to improve your control as well as enable you to make passes on your competitors and improve your lap times. It must also be stressed that charging too fast into a corner and then simply braking as hard and as late as possible is not always going to reduce your lap time. Under most situations, braking should be carried out smoothly and in a straight line where the car is less likely to break traction, slide, and possibly spin out. With an

electric-powered model there is some degree of natural braking effect from the motor, and this will help to control the corner speed. With a nitro-powered model, though, braking is used a lot more due to the clutch, as the car will tend to coast easier and you'll need to apply the brakes before entering a corner.

When using the brakes, make sure that you're on the right line as you approach the corner and apply the brakes smoothly until you've reduced your speed by the required amount. You should then turn the car in towards the apex of the corner, once again keeping all the steering inputs smooth and using the minimum amount of steering lock – too much steering lock will slow you down. Once you've reached the apex you can begin to reapply the throttle, keeping the steering angle consistent as you try to open up the corner as much as possible and increasing the throttle application without breaking traction by spinning the wheels.

If you're overtaking someone on a corner the same principle of braking and turning in applies, but

BOTTOM LEFT Braking is a skill to be learnt as you try to slow the model down quickly but in a controlled manner. If you're too heavy on the brakes the model can become unstable, as in this instance.

LEFT Making a pass on another car starts by pulling alongside and taking up the space that your competitor (the blue car) needs. You'll then effectively block the perfect line, although it'll be necessary to make a more aggressive turn because of the narrower entry. As your competitor's line has been compromised, you'll be able to hit the clipping point on the exit and complete your move.

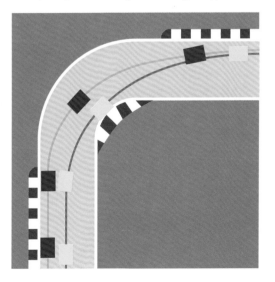

ABOVE Generally a little wheelspin is no bad thing, but be careful to apply the throttle steadily and smoothly without being reckless.

bear in mind that you won't be on the perfect line so you'll have to make a much tighter turn to get round the corner. Most corner-overtaking manoeuvres are actually made by getting 'inside' the car ahead, which then puts your car in a position where you're able to prevent your opponent from taking the perfect line. Remember that you then don't need to get past the other car, as just being alongside it will be perfect.

Although we've mentioned the principle of braking in a straight line and then letting off as you turn in, there are a few exceptions where you can learn a skill that will help you in the future. For example, if you turn the steering whilst you're braking the car may be provoked into a slide. Getting the car to slide in off-road racing is very common, since, just as in full-size rallying, a slide can help you to get round the corner quicker. When the grip is good you may find that you either need to grab the brakes hard whilst steering to create a slide, or be brutal with the controls. This kind of effect helps the car to pivot in a corner and is often used when the car is understeering and you need to make it turn.

In slippery conditions when the grip levels aren't ideal you may find yourself having to use the brakes more often to slow the car down and make it steer better for the corners. You'll need to find a suitable balance, though, as using the brakes can tend to increase your chances of losing control, by locking the wheels for example.

Throttle application

Like any form of motor sport, throttle application in RC is important in controlling the vehicle and will help to prolong the life of your equipment. In most situations, and especially on-road racing, your throttle application should be smooth and not so aggressive that the wheels spin and you lose control. Spinning the wheels obviously means that you're not getting the power to the track and you're potentially damaging the tyres. In off-road racing, though, getting the wheels to spin can help you to improve lap times and is virtually impossible to avoid when you're driving on low grip or loose surfaces.

Whatever form of car racing you participate in, good driving techniques are the key to success. The most expensive motor, chassis or tyres are useless unless their advantages can be applied in a smooth and professional way. Good driving can only be explained in strict terms. What's far more educational is to watch other drivers at the local club. Try to watch the guys who win regularly and see how they take the corners. They're sure not to be the most spectacular, but they'll almost certainly be the smoothest.

Mastering jumps

What's the secret to a perfect leap? Special shock absorber oil? Extra bouncy springs? Super high-grip tyres? Actually, it's mostly down to your use of the throttle!

Few aspects of the hobby are more exciting than leaping an RC vehicle. Jumps, somersaults and back-flips not only look spectacular, but they also provide an immediate adrenalin buzz, especially when you complete the giant leap with a perfect four-wheel landing. However, while today's

RC kits are specifically designed to take a huge amount of punishment they still have their limitations. An ugly crash can break things. In competition, a reckless roll can lose you the race. Master the technique of jumping properly and such events can be avoided; but what exactly *is* the secret to achieving a perfect leap?

The simple answer is that it's all about increasing or reducing the amount of throttle and timing. Due to the torque reaction of the motor and wheels, the attitude of your RC car or truck can actually be adjusted while it's in the air by applying small throttle and brake movements via the transmitter. Hit the throttle in mid-air and your model will raise its nose. Jab the brakes and it'll nosedive. If the chassis is level, hold the throttle where it is and you'll be poised for a perfect landing.

Race technique

Of course, the aesthetic result you're aiming to achieve changes depending on whether you're racing your truck or just having some fun. If you're racing, your truck will travel far quicker when the four tyres are in contact with the track and the engine is pushing them along. So while it may look spectacular to jump higher and further than everyone else, minimising the amount of airtime will result in faster lap times. Keeping the jump low and landing quickly will ensure minimal time is lost during the jump itself, and once back on the ground the truck will accelerate again.

Staying stuck to the track isn't always the best tactic, though. Sometimes big jumps can save you time, especially when you come across several obstacles together. A 'double jump', for example, is

often best cleared quickly by accelerating hard over the first hump, before landing on the down section of the last. Consistency is important too. In a race situation one small crash can cost you a lot of time, so be prepared to drive at less than 100 per cent if it allows you to keep your model out of trouble and take the jumps safely. If leaping the first jump will cause your car or truck to land on the top of the next ramp the landing will be very unstable, so reduce the power, run over the first ramp smoothly, and then accelerate into the final jump. When racing there's little point in blasting a series of jumps in an attempt to gain a few seconds only to lose that time and more by cartwheeling off to one side.

ABOVE For the best control during flight try to keep your car or truck flat whilst jumping. *(www.oople.com)*

BELOW During racing your lines may have to change, so be aware that the jumps may be slightly different too, as the take-off section may not be the same across its width. *(Thorsten Gora)*

ABOVE When a car bottoms out the chassis hits the ground and the suspension has no effect. It's easy to lose control when a car bottoms out on either take-off or landing.

Perfect start, perfect ending

The ending of a leap is largely decided by the way it started. A perfect ending occurs when the four wheels hit the ground at a similar time, ideally with the vehicle's nose level or pointing slightly upwards. To achieve this it's important to enter the ramp cleanly with the appropriate amount of throttle. First, you need a straight line going into the jump. Remember that this is a car, not an aeroplane; once take-off has been achieved the direction the model will head in has largely been decided. If it's sliding sideways or is about to roll on entry, then it's highly likely to end up in an even bigger mess when it comes off the ramp. To avoid a tumble, ease back on the throttle to settle the

suspension and try to hit the jump square on, not at an angle. Once on the jump face, accelerate up it and then release the throttle as the model takes off. This standard technique works especially well on large, smooth jumps, such as the artificial obstacles often used on temporary circuits. The suspension compresses on the ramp and helps to push the car or truck off the end. Aim to leave the jump off-power, as the energy absorbed by the ramp will stop the nose from launching too high into the air.

Don't be afraid of speed. Speed adds distance to the jump and the longer your RC vehicle stays in the air the more time you get to make adjustments with the throttle. Drive too slowly up a ramp and your vehicle is certain to nosedive. Leap quickly off the jump face and regardless of the exit angle you can often still rectify things by using the throttle to alter the model's attitude while it's in the air. If your car or truck jumps nose high, hitting the brakes in mid-air will stop the driven wheels from spinning and will cause its nose to drop down. Conversely, hitting the throttle in mid-air will cause it to lift.

Changing your vehicle's side-to-side angle is trickier, but if it's leaning to one side you can make some adjustment in the air using the steering. Simply steer into the direction of the lean – for example, if it's leaning to the left, steer left. But make sure you release the steering again before landing or your cunning stunt will end with an unpleasant high-speed roll.

With all jumps, wait until all four wheels are safely on the ground before you apply the throttle again. Slamming the power on when only the rear wheels have touched down will make the model wheelie and it will quickly become unstable.

A common mistake

The most frequent mistake made by beginners is to attempt to extend the distance of a jump by slamming the throttle forward once the vehicle is in the air. This doesn't work. By the time the car or truck has left the ramp, the distance it will travel has already been set. Accelerating now will simply lift the nose. Attempt a severe nose-up landing and the back wheels will touch down first, the front will flip backwards, and your vehicle will skid along on its roof. Of course, the suspension can't fully absorb the impact of the landing when the vehicle tips upside down, so it's no surprise that a backwards landing is one of the mishaps that's most likely to cause damage.

Tabletops

Some jumps are designed with a central plateau or 'tabletop'. The technique for leaping these

RIGHT Jumping with the throttle still applied will see the nose point upwards, which is not good technique. (www.oople.com)

depends on the length of the level section of the jump. If this is short you can simply treat it as a regular leap, but if it's long ease off the throttle on entry and smoothly climb up to the tabletop. The throttle can then be applied as you commence the downward slope, leaping off the end of the table and hopefully landing on all four wheels.

Multiple bumps

Multiple small jumps can be more of a problem since their severity can be difficult to assess from the drivers' rostrum. Taking small jumps with the power applied can help as it keeps the nose in the air and prevents it from nose-diving into the ground. Try out different racing lines if there are a lot of small obstacles. There's usually at least one line that's better than all the others, one that will allow you to miss the worst bumps or hold the power on for longer.

Use the brakes

Using the brakes is an important aspect of driving as it helps to control your car or truck on the ground and in the air. The braking set-up is vital, as too much braking will cause the model to spin and too little will make you slow around the track. The relative braking power also reflects how a model will react in the air, as sudden, hard braking has a more noticeable effect than smooth brake application.

Safety first

It should go without saying, but always jump your RC model somewhere safe, away from other people and their property. No matter how expert you are, jumping is not a precise science and crashes will undoubtedly happen. Damaging your model car or truck may only cost a few pounds to

fix but third party insurance claims can end up costing millions.

Plenty of practice

Practice is the real key to successful jumping. Changing shock absorber settings and weight distribution can gradually improve your vehicle's jumping ability, but driving it better will have a much bigger effect. Attempt the same jump again and again and learn how to use the throttle to control your model's behaviour, both on entry to the jump and while it's in the air. Tap the brakes in mid-air to bring the nose down, or, if the nose is too low, blip the throttle to raise it. You won't get it right every time, but you'll soon learn what works and what doesn't. And of course, you'll have heaps of fun at the same time.

ABOVE Keep the speed to a minimum so that the landing is made with the greatest control. *(www.oople.com)*

FAR LEFT If the model's nose is up during flight you'll need to apply the brakes.

LEFT Alternatively, if the nose is pointing down use the throttle aggressively to bring the front up.

Problem solving

Glitches

Whatever level you compete at, experiencing
intermittent radio interference is a sure way of your
race day being ruined. Making a mistake in your
fastest qualifying run might be annoying; being
bundled off the circuit by a throttle-crazed racer
even more so. But for a really annoying racing
experience, there's one clear winner – radio
interference. Suffer from the dreaded 'glitches' and
your entire race meeting can be ruined as you
remain in control of the car for some laps and
periodically lose control on others. Sometimes the
interference only occurs at specific parts of the
circuit and often only at really inopportune
moments, such as when you're dicing for position
or being lapped by the race leader. But while the
glitches themselves might be annoying, the ensuing
search for the root cause can be both frustrating
and time consuming, requiring a combination of
systematic elimination and 'trial and error' to
discover a cure.

A radio 'glitch' is clearly different to having
someone switch on a transmitter using the same
frequency as your own. If this happens, you soon
know about it since your car rapidly becomes
completely uncontrollable. Instead, a glitch is
typically defined as an unwanted event that occurs
over a short period of time; an event that can't be
easily repeated. In a radio control car that means an
errant electronic signal occurs that causes the radio
equipment to respond, a signal that was definitely
not generated by the driver's own movements on
the transmitter controls. The good news is that
there's a genuine reason why most glitches occur.
The bad news is that it can take some time to find
it. So in order to help that process, here's our guide
to the ten most common causes of radio glitches:

Unreliable connections

Intermittent electrical contact can generate power
spikes and cause glitches, and the main culprits
are usually dodgy connectors or poor solder joints.
Finding the exact problem area can prove difficult,
not least because what may appear to be a reliable
connection while the car is stationary may prove to
be less so when it's hurtling round the racetrack.
Dry solder joints are the first obvious targets to look
for. Check all leads to ensure the soldered
connections are firm and aren't liable to break apart
when the wire's given a sharp tug. Then check the
connectors themselves to ensure they fit together
securely and don't shake about. The plugs into
the receiver are prime candidates to check,
particularly when mixing a receiver and servos from
different manufacturers.

Receiver aerial route

The way the aerial has been routed in the car will
affect its sensitivity. The intent should always be for
the receiver aerial to go up and out of the car as
quickly as possible, keeping it well away from the
conductive metal or carbon-fibre found on the
chassis. If the receiver aerial is too long, it should
never *ever* be cut. The length of the aerial is
accurately calculated for each make of receiver,
and for maximum sensitivity it must remain at
exactly that size. Since aerials are usually longer
than the accompanying aerial tubes, most drivers
make small neat coils of the remaining wire on top
of the receiver. Others go one better and use an

internal antenna loom that ensures the aerial never loops over itself. Moving the receiver around in the car or mounting it on its side are other tricks that can help to ensure a reliable radio signal is received.

Lead length

Keeping the lengths of radio leads to a minimum can eliminate the need to loop and tie them together, and allows them to be more neatly routed in the car. Most top racers trim and re-solder the servo and speed control leads so that there's just enough slack to allow the removal of these without straining the connections. With older equipment for which the warranty has expired, an even neater rewiring job can be performed by dismantling the unit and re-soldering the wire at the circuit-board end. Don't attempt to change the lengths of radio leads unless you're proficient at soldering, though. You might eliminate the glitches caused by unnecessarily long and looped leads, but introduce glitches caused by unreliable connections.

Motor arcing

In an electric car, many of the unwanted radio frequencies are generated by the motor. In a brushed motor the brushes can actually touch the same segment of the rotating commutator during each revolution. This causes a short circuit for an instant in time and the motor will arc as a result of the current flowing through the copper. This arcing happens for a split second but can occur nearly 50,000 times per minute, and this creates an electrical noise that can affect the receiver. To suppress these noises, small ceramic capacitors are soldered to the motor's endbell. On some modified motors these come pre-installed; on others they'll be included in the packet and require soldering into position. Use a hot soldering iron to do this and keep the capacitor legs as short as possible to ensure they don't catch on the chassis when the motor is installed. Whenever you remove the motor from your car, check the capacitors to ensure they remain firmly soldered in place. A dry solder joint on one of the legs can be enough to cause major radio interference. Many high-frequency, forward-only electronic speed controls also require a Schottky diode to be fitted, which further isolates high voltage spikes.

Brushless motor technology brings with it an arc-free environment since it avoids the brush/commutator interface that's otherwise the source of arcing with brushed motors. Remember also that when using brushed motors the commutator and brush interface can become damaged over time due to overheating of the motor

or brush wear. This can promote a type of micro-vibration called brush bounce, whereby the commutator surface becomes warped and the brush can't maintain a consistent electrical contact. This bouncing creates arcing and electrical noise, so if your brushed motor is old and you haven't cleaned it, replaced the brushes, or had it skimmed and rebuilt, it may be that it's the cause of any newfound unwanted glitching.

Receiver voltage

All receivers only operate correctly when they receive an input voltage in the manufacturer-specified range. If the input voltage gets too low glitches can occur. When running your car off an external receiver battery pack the cells must therefore be fresh or recently charged. In an electric car where the power comes from the main battery pack itself, the appropriate elimination circuitry must be used. Modern electronic speed controls have such voltage regulators built in and will ensure the radio equipment is always given priority over the supply of power to the motor.

ABOVE Without the capacitors and Schottky diode fitted there's a chance of increased motor arcing, which will cause increased wear on the commutator and possible interference.

BELOW An electrical switch like this one from KO Propo features an indicator to show the status of the receiver pack's voltage.

ABOVE There are times that your position on the rostrum can cause interference, so be prepared to move.

frequencies that are very close to the others in use in a race. A slightly out of tune transmitter, running on a frequency close to your own, can cause signals that get picked up by your own car. For that reason most race directors try to leave a 'double gap' of frequencies in each race, ensuring a good spread across the available range. They may be less likely to do this for the finals, though, so check the listing when it's posted and ask to change frequency if you end up immediately adjacent to another. Frequency monitors are available that can detect when a transmitter is giving out a rogue signal and these are used at major meetings when a driver complains about radio interference before the start of a race.

Transmitter problems

It should go without saying that the transmitter itself should be in perfect working order complete with a fully charged battery. Checking the voltage on the meter provides a quick way to verify this. To find out whether the radio equipment itself is the cause of your 'glitches', replace the transmitter and receiver with the combination from one of your other cars. Alternatively, borrow a unit from another driver. If the car doesn't glitch with the new equipment you can be pretty sure the original combination is at fault. It can be repaired by returning it to the authorised distributor, together with a detailed letter explaining the exact problem. Make sure you get a quote for the required work first so that there are no financial surprises.

Rostrum position

Moving positions on the rostrum might sound like a dubious cure, but it's amazing how many times this can work. If the glitch only occurs at one particular point on the race circuit, only when you're standing next to a particular driver, or only when you're driving under the transmitter aerials of other drivers, then changing positions can provide a simple cure. There's usually a more logical reason why your receiver is proving to be particularly sensitive to the signals generated by other transmitters, but this is one of the few cures you can attempt during a race. The other is to consciously change the angle at which you're holding the transmitter aerial, ensuring it points upwards rather than down into the ground.

Frequency choice

While occasionally caused by a damaged crystal, most frequency-related glitches occur when running

Other drivers

Occasionally it may not be your car or radio equipment that's at fault. Some drivers have been known to boost the power output of their transmitter by adding extra cells, a practice that's specifically outlawed by the British Radio Car Association (BRCA). Consequently some sections' rules allow the race director to randomly ask competitors to open their transmitter case to prove they're not cheating in this way. Some drivers have also been caught running illegal frequencies outside the approved range, again, if the race director detects such activity the punishment is usually instant disqualification.

External radio signals

If you're racing near power lines or a radio or television transmitter there's a chance that the other radio signals in the area may be so strong that your receiver isn't able to reject them. We've even seen instances where the public address system used at a race has caused cars to glitch! Thankfully, outside interference of this kind is relatively rare and can

RIGHT Radio masts and telegraph poles can be a potential cause of radio problems.

sometimes be cured by switching off the offending item when that's possible. In the worst cases, however, you'll need to change the location of your race and move to an area where the only signals generated are those from the radio control transmitters.

Avoiding interference

Interference is what happens when an outside influence affects the control of an RC vehicle. For example, the steering sometimes moves when you're going in a straight line, or your car or truck may stutter under acceleration. This can be very frustrating, and although it's sometimes avoidable there are a number of ways to avoid getting it in the first place.

The chances of interference happening are greater when you're in a confined area such as a racetrack or when there are multiple RC users around. The simplest solution to two people attempting to use the same frequency at the same time is the 'peg board', variations of which are seen at most clubs across the country. The principle is very straightforward. Before you switch on your transmitter you first collect a wooden clothes peg corresponding to your frequency from a board next to the drivers' rostrum. You clip this peg on your transmitter and only then are you allowed to switch it on. Once you've finished racing, you switch everything off and place the peg back on the board. If a driver goes to collect a specific peg and it isn't there, it indicates that someone else is already using that frequency. Therefore the driver must either wait for the current user to finish, or change to another frequency. Of course, it requires discipline from all the drivers for this system to work well, but it's been used at many, many meetings over the years with considerable success.

Direct Sequencing Spread Spectrum

The advent of Direct Sequencing Spread Spectrum technology, operating on 2.4GHz, is proving to be an enormous leap forward in the battle against radio interference. Not only does this technology automatically search and allocate a 'safe' operating frequency for the transmitter and receiver pairing, but since it's operating on a very high frequency it virtually eliminates all on-car sources of interference from arcing motors or metal vibrations.

Mechanical shocks

It goes without saying that no RC equipment likes being mechanically abused or damaged in any way. Whilst the transmitter itself is relatively safe in

your hands, the equipment in the car is often subjected to a harsh existence of sudden shocks that can shorten its life. In electric cars the receiver is always mounted directly onto the chassis by means of self-adhesive tape, but experienced drivers of nitro cars prefer wrapping the receiver in foam without securing it directly to the receiver box. This isolates it from much of the engine-induced vibration whilst giving it good protection against the sudden impacts created when jumping or driving over bumpy tracks. Failure to provide sufficient vibration isolation can lead, very quickly, to unseen damage to the crystal in particular, which will cause radio interference. Likewise, failure to store your crystals safely, or dropping them onto a hard surface, will damage them internally and necessitate replacement. With care crystals will last an incredibly long time, but they're easily damaged if not handled correctly.

ABOVE The 2.4GHz band has proved to be a good way of avoiding radio interference from other drivers.

BELOW Pack your receiver box out with foam so that it doesn't get thrown around inside during use.

7

Going racing

Finding out more – the next steps	**131**
Race day	**133**
The racing classes	**135**

Photo: (Adrian Svensson)

So you're thinking of going racing? Sounds simple doesn't it? – grab your car and your transmitter and off you go. Easy! Well, it can be that easy, but in reality it usually requires a degree of research and preparation before you get to that point.

ABOVE Racing gets the adrenalin pumping as you compete wheel-to-wheel against other cars, plan your fuel-stop strategy and pull overtaking moves.

Most people start off in RC with little or no idea of the extent of competitive racing that exists, from local level 'club' racing through national points series to international Grands Prix, and culminating in biennial World Championship events. Indeed, there are myriads of different types of model and corresponding race classes, from ultra-small 1:16 and 1:18 micro electric racers to huge 1:5 scale petrol-engine powered touring car and outlaw classes.

As with full-sized motor sport, each RC class has its own rules and regulations, laying down the overall construction parameters for the models and defining the rules for racing. Most types of organised competition follow the principles laid down by national bodies such as the UK's BRCA. Depending on class there'll be subtle differences between the actual race rules, but by and large every class adopts a race format that consists of a series of timed qualifying heats and a series of seeded finals. The objective is to complete as

many fast laps as possible during your heat (which normally lasts five minutes), so that you become 'seeded' into a final alongside other drivers who've achieved similar times on the day. In all cases qualifying takes place alongside other drivers, not in isolation, so both race etiquette and racing skills are factors as you attempt to negotiate the track and outwit your rivals without losing time in unnecessary collisions and accidents. Quite often individually very fast drivers fail to dominate proceedings on the track because they don't have the mental strength to drive in constant close proximity to other cars and drivers.

All this adds to the adrenalin and excitement that racing provides, and, along with the camaraderie and laughter, is why many RC enthusiasts are drawn irresistibly towards the racing scene.

Finding out more – the next steps

Traditionally, the best source of information about your local race scene has always been the local model shop. Staffed by like-minded enthusiasts, this provides a social venue for local racers and is a

veritable goldmine of real-world information. Radio control magazines are also a useful source and provide a market-wide snapshot of current products and trends, along with helpful tips and 'how-to' articles. Increasingly, however, the internet is

ABOVE You can learn a great deal at grass roots level: a local club will give you the chance to race against drivers of many different levels.

LEFT Specialist magazines offer lots of information about racing, including event reports, forthcoming race dates, set-up information and news of the latest products and kits.

experience at a local club before they start to travel further afield.

Again, your best sources of information are likely to be your local model shop and the internet. Websites such as the BRCA's www.brca.org and forums such as www.rcracechat.com provide listings and contact details for known clubs in your locality.

These days most commercially available RC cars conform to the regulations of their respective race classes and could be raced straight from the box, but as you become more involved in racing you'll begin to appreciate the need for some of the accessories and upgrades that are available. But, as with any type of sport or hobby, the acquisition of accessories won't automatically improve your lap times and race pace. Only patience and practice will do that.

Don't panic!

Going racing for the very first time can be quite daunting. Nervousness, the fear of not knowing what to do and ignorance of the required protocol can all be rather intimidating, but, with a little bit of preparation much of this can be easily overcome.

Once you've decided where you'd like to race, contact one of the club officials and discuss your situation with them. Explain that you're new to the sport and that you don't know what to expect or do. Don't worry – all club officials are enthusiasts themselves and will understand what you're feeling. Speaking to someone beforehand, whether by email or telephone, means that by the time you go

ABOVE A trackside shop will carry specific items suited to the track where they're based, but usually they also have a local permanent base where they carry greater stock and more variety.

becoming an important source of information, as manufacturers, distributors and retailers all vie for your surfing attention, whilst RC-orientated user forums provide details of racers' actual experiences.

Which class?

The various existing classes are explained on page 135 Inevitably, deciding which one to race in will largely depend upon whether you already own a suitable type of car and what class actually appeals to you the most. In many instances another significant factor will be the presence of a suitable local venue, as most people begin their racing

BELOW Don't get blown away by the choice of classes – make rational decisions based on what you want to race, the kind of tracks accessible to you, and how supportive your local model shop is.

to the track you'll already be feeling less intimidated. Arrange to meet your contact at the track, and when you arrive ask for him by name. You'll soon be pointed in the right direction – but remember, race meetings can be quite frantic at times, and if he appears to be very busy the chances are that he'll find it difficult to devote much time to introductions. For this reason it's almost always best to go to the club on an occasion *before* you intend to race, so that you can observe how things are run and familiarise yourself with the proceedings.

Race day

It goes without saying that a good day's racing starts with a lot of preparation – both for you and your car. Whether electric or nitro, off-road or on-road, we all need some form of power supply, whether it's to charge batteries, receiver packs, transmitters or just soldering irons. The racers' favourite is the good old 12V battery, since not many tracks – especially outdoor ones here in the UK – have mains power supply, and we therefore have to take our own. A 12V battery comes in all shapes and sizes, from a basic motorcycle battery right up to the largest leisure battery. The basic principle is: the bigger the battery the longer it will last between charges, an important factor if you're considering doing a two-day meeting away from home. With careful treatment most batteries can last at least a couple of years before requiring replacement.

Personal comfort

All of us who already race will have pitted from the back of our car at some time – and it's not very comfortable, believe me! The widely used folding picnic table is a good solution: compact, relatively lightweight, and at a squeeze suitable for a couple of drivers. If you're after a bit more room most DIY stores now stock a robust version of the wallpaper-pasting table, which, combined with a folding chair, will provide both space and comfort.

You'll also need to think about some sort of weather protection if you're racing outdoors. With the unpredictability of British weather you'll need an

ABOVE At the track, you can talk to the organisers and get background information about how the meetings are run, as well as advice on car requirements and other useful information. Once you feel ready, hand over your entry fee and you can get on the track.

LEFT Preparation is the key. Make sure you have all the things you think you may need, but don't worry if you can't afford everything – there are always other racers who'll help you out with parts, accessories, tools and, most importantly, advice.

ABOVE There's a drivers' briefing at all meetings, from club races through to major international events. These will tell you where everything is and provide details of the schedule.

A typical day's club racing

You normally arrive trackside at about breakfast time and unload and set up your racing gear, pit table and chair, along with your 12V, tools and batteries if it's an electric meeting, fuel and fuel bottle if it's nitro. The track will normally be open for practice whilst the Race Director books drivers in. Practice normally finishes when all the drivers have been booked in and a heat listing produced. Most classes then go through three or four rounds of qualifying – that is, racing against the clock to

establish the final grid positions. Once qualifying has finished the lap timing system produces a finals listing. Drivers who are in the finals then race against each other for position, points and championships. The top finalists, racing in the A Final, may have to race more than one leg, their final positions being decided by a points system. After that the awards are presented if there are any, and, if it's a big meeting, photos are taken. Then you pack up and wind your weary way home – hopefully clutching a trophy!

RIGHT If you get an opportunity, walk the track before the race so that you can look for lines, spot bumps and gain as much knowledge as possible before you get onto the drivers' rostrum.

umbrella, E-Z Up shelter, tent or, ultimately, a caravan with an awning to keep dry in the pits. As for warmth in the winter, don't forget to take warm clothing, waterproofs and even gloves. Transmitter warmers can also be useful in the depths of winter, as your hands and also your potentially very expensive transmitter will otherwise be exposed to the elements. Even if you're racing indoors, it may still be cold in the winter, so be prepared.

A lot of tracks are in or surrounded by potentially muddy fields, so taking boots of some description to change into may also prove useful.

The inner self

It sounds ridiculous, but with everything else that's going on during a race day it's easy to forget about your own needs, particularly in the food and drink department. Most, if not all, of the bigger events are geared to provide refreshments, normally in the shape of a trusty burger van, some of which are good, others less so! Most smaller events, however, won't even have this facility, so check if you need to take your own supplies or else find out where the nearest fast food outlet or petrol station is situated.

The racing classes

Micro – small but perfectly formed

This is one of the newest classes of RC racing and caters for almost all off-road cars, buggies, stadium trucks and monster trucks from 1:16 to

1:18 scale. It's a very cheap form of racing, with the top drivers using the same sort of vehicle as competitors who've never driven before, the only differences being experience and car set-up.

Micro racing is relaxed and fun, with drivers smiling as they come off the rostrum even after a bad race, having had the fun of jumping an eight-inch car six feet in the air and performing awesome wall rides. And it's nearly as much fun to watch as it is to race.

Although it's quite new, micro racing interest is huge and most manufacturers produce cars or hop-ups for the most popular chassis, two of

ABOVE A chair, pit table and shelter will make your day much more comfortable, particularly during inclement weather.

LEFT Micro racing is one of the newer classes. It provides all the thrill of electric off-road racing action – but indoors. *(Cris Oxley)*

ABOVE 1:12 scale is arguably the purest form of RC racing, with its foam tyres, high levels of grip and – at eight-minutes per qualifier and final – the longest electric races in the hobby.

these being the Associated RC18 and the FTX Blaze, both of these can be raced straight from the box. There's also a wealth of trackside knowledge available to help newcomers set up their cars.

For further information, and to see the cars in action, follow the 'Micro' links on the BRCA website.

1:12 On-Road – precision personified

A perfect-handling 1:12 scale car is a dream to drive. Anyone who's driven one will tell you this, and many feel that this class represents one of the purest forms of RC racing.

The 1:12 class started back in 1975, when Tamiya created it by releasing a kit with a simple chassis, six cells, and an awesome set of Porsche sports car bodies. By the early 1980s it had become hugely popular, Mardave, Lectricar and Schumacher all starting their businesses by producing 1:12 scale cars.

When Tamiya released the Sand Scorcher off-road buggy in the early 1990s many people rushed off to join this new class, leaving 1:12 with few drivers and even less choice of cars. For the next ten years it languished, buoyed principally by its IFMAR World Championship status, before it changed to a four-cell format and underwent a huge revival. Today, with more cars than ever, much lower costs than 1:10 touring cars, and its focus on drivers' skills rather than the depth of their pockets, this class is the best in electric RC racing.

The design of a 1:12 scale chassis is enshrined in the rules, and little has changed in the past 20 years. This has allowed not just big manufacturers such as Associated, Hot Bodies, Yokomo, CRC,

Trinity and Corally to produce cars, but a whole slew of smaller companies too. This huge variety, with cars costing between £100 and £200, is what makes the 1:12 class so interesting.

The cars are of a simple design but use the latest materials, such as carbon fibre and titanium. This makes them very lightweight, which is what gives them their incredible speed and acceleration and makes them probably the fastest of any of the electric racing classes. They're powered by rechargeable batteries, with electronic speed control and a small electric motor providing the drive to the rear wheels.

They can be raced outdoors on tarmac tracks, this being the norm in sunnier parts of the world such as Japan and the US, but here in the UK 1:12 racing more usually takes place indoors during the winter on a special carpet surface. The cars use foam tyres that give them amazing levels of grip in the corners, making them real fun to drive. There are a large number of BRCA-affiliated 1:12 clubs throughout the country, and to be able to race indoors in the warm and dry on a cold winter's day has to be a major attraction. Unlike the other electric classes 1:12 races are eight minutes in length, and this increased track time for your money and the relatively low cost of running 1:12 scale circuit cars have to be the class's other major advantages.

Today 1:12 remains RC's best-kept secret. Results depend 80 per cent on driver skill, 10 per cent on the car and 10 per cent on set-up. Costs are the lowest of any RC electric class, especially for motors, batteries and chassis parts. There's a huge range of cars to choose from, yet only one body style, and only a couple of tyre compounds are needed in order to compete anywhere. Tuning is about adjustment and knowledge, not buying parts.

Driving a car at up to 35mph, where a corner has to be completed in less than a second, and you race inches from the car in front, brings out the best drivers in the world. Every National has a final that'll make you leap from your seat with excitement, and Britain boasts the best 1:12 driver ever – reigning World Champion David Spashett.

Mardave V12 and Mini-stock – bash and crash

One of the original founding electric chassis manufacturers, Mardave's V12 and Mini-stock cars enjoy a loyal following of novice and hardened oval enthusiasts alike.

Whilst many forms of RC racing are intended to be non-contact, the Mini-stock scene is, in its truest sense, a miniaturised version of full-sized oval banger racing. The appeal of the class lies in its minimum cost approach, as expensive options and upgrades are outlawed to help prevent the spiralling costs so prevalent in other classes. A simple four-cell NiMH battery powers a stock 540-sized Mabuchi motor that's directly driven to a solid axle at the rear. A simple sprung front axle and a floating rear motor sub-chassis provide limited and crude but effective suspension.

Raced exclusively indoors, the Mardave class is often supported by local clubs in order to encourage younger drivers into RC racing, as it can provide a fantastically simple yet durable chassis that's immensely strong.

1:10 Touring Car – tour to victory

Electric touring car racing is one of the most accessible classes, with race meetings often held during the week as well as at weekends. With a choice of categories to suit performance and budget, there's sure to be something that suits you.

Introduced more than a decade ago, 1:10 scale electric-powered touring cars have brought the thrills and spills of the full-sized series onto smaller scale racetracks around the world, and with a multitude of new products still being released every month that enthusiasm shows no signs of diminishing.

Today's electric-powered touring cars are the most technically advanced, reliable and highest performing vehicles ever. Almost all of the major model car manufacturers cater for this class, resulting in a mind-boggling variety of choice. In a sport where you can decide how serious and

expensive you want the racing to become, fun is guaranteed wherever you decide to take your car. From thrashing around the driveway at home to competing at the local club or in international competitions, the cars are all designed to be raced and enjoyed.

All manner of drive systems, body styles, weight distributions and levels of adjustability are available, enabling every aspiring racer to select a car best suited to their own requirements. Race results suggest that belt-drive models are best suited to high-powered modified motors, while shaft-drive models work particularly well with slower stock motors.

ABOVE Many racers start out competing mid-week with one of Mardave's popular cars. The V12 and Mini cars are cheap to buy, inexpensive to run and loads of fun. Their small size makes them ideal for small village halls where space is at a premium.
(Jon Painter)

LEFT With their Lexan bodyshells and bright paint schemes, touring cars offer a great visual display when they go wheel to wheel. Their 4WD transmissions, carbon fibre, titanium and alloy components and brushless motor systems also make them extremely technical and rewarding cars to drive.

RIGHT Surface changes, track degradation, changing weather and a whole range of set-up options combine to make off-road racing a real test of both your driving skills and your ability to tune the car to conditions.

Electric-powered cars are equally at home racing outdoors on tarmac or indoors on carpet or polished wood. Thanks to their lightweight construction they corner very quickly, and on a small track are even capable of outperforming the nitro-powered cars. Rechargeable cells provide run times in excess of five minutes and super-quick acceleration, while the fastest cars can top 50mph. The cells can be recharged in around 45 minutes using a special charger connected to a 12V car battery or suitable mains adapter.

1:10 Off-Road – ten-tenths

The off-road scene is still highly regarded, with its demands on both set-up and driving skills on tracks that generally change throughout the course of a meeting.

Most 1:10 off-road models are purchased in kit form and can be built in a matter of hours. They include fully independent suspension, with interchangeable oils and springs for fine-tuning opportunities. Six rechargeable batteries are used to power a noise-free electric motor. Drivers race for five-minute periods to achieve their best possible result by means of both their driving skills and their set-up capabilities.

The last few years have witnessed the re-emergence of 1:10 off-road electric buggies. Their simplicity, ease of build and set-up, and lower maintenance and start-up costs have led quite naturally to a huge influx of new drivers into this two-wheel-drive class. However, manufacturers are quite limited, with Associated and Losi being the most popular.

Until very recently all the cars followed the same format of rear wheels driven by a gear-type differential hanging out of the back of the buggy, but then X Factory released its X-6 with the motor and gearbox located between the front and rear wheels. At the time of writing a basic but competent 2WD buggy can be purchased for as little as £70, or even less, but top competition buggies with the latest high-quality, technologically advanced chassis will set you back in excess of £200. If you want to get into 1:10 electric off-road racing we would recommend a 2WD to start with, but some people would argue that the true definition of a 1:10 off-road buggy is one that has four-wheel drive.

The massive worldwide resurgence of the 1:10 electric off-road classes has resulted in a cavalcade of new 4WD chassis being released, most notably during the last 12 months. Even excluding prototypes, custom-built specials and one-off home-grown chassis there are still more than ten different 4WD chassis available!

2WD and 4WD buggies are designed for many surfaces, so tracks are built on grass, dirt, Astroturf, tarmac or a mixture of surfaces. There are jumps and bumps to test a driver's skill and ability to the full, while humps, hollows, camber changes and a fast straight make for a perfect day's racing.

1:10 IC –
tear up the tarmac

If you want to race at the fastest possible speed then look no further than 1:8 nitro-powered circuit cars, but never forget that their slightly smaller 1:10

LEFT These 200mm-wide 1:10 touring cars are powered by a small .12ci engine, although with foam tyres and a two-speed gearbox you can be sure of impressive acceleration and top speeds.

ABOVE 1:10 nitro trucks offer high performance from a relatively simple platform. Look out for a growing range of kits in both two- and four-wheel-drive formats.

scale relatives pack a mean punch too. Their biggest difference from an electric-powered racer becomes apparent as soon as you first drive a nitro-powered circuit car. Running on special nitro fuel, they sound and smell just like real racing cars and have an absolutely incredible amount of power. Top speeds in excess of 65mph are common with competition-orientated racers, as are run times of around ten minutes. Extending the runtime further is simply a matter of pulling into the pit lane, topping up the fuel tank, and accelerating away once more – just like a Formula One fuel stop in miniature.

However, while the scream of the nitro engine undoubtedly adds extra excitement, it also limits the number of places in which you can use the car. Some clubs have to comply with noise restrictions imposed by the local council and may not even support the use of nitro-powered machines, so always check first before you make a purchase.

If you do decide to go nitro racing, then it's a good idea to persuade a friend to get involved too, since you'll need someone to fuel your car before the qualifying run, to hold the car at the start of the race, to refuel it during the final and to restart it if it stalls. It also helps to have someone to share ideas and skills with; multi-speed gearboxes, glow plugs, air filters, tuned silencers, mechanical brakes – underneath that bodyshell there's a whole lot of interesting technology you'll have to learn about!

The 1:10 nitro class has grown rapidly over the past five years and is now supported by many of the largest RC manufacturers. The cars are highly adjustable, extremely fast and perfectly suited to the purpose-built RC race circuits found across Europe. Equally capable on foam or rubber tyres, they're at their most popular when racing on moulded rubber tyres using 200mm-wide touring car bodyshells.

1:10 Truck – muscular hardware

Why trucks? Well, of all the off-road RC disciplines truck driving is the most fun. Why? Because with the possible exception of 1:8 rallycross nothing jumps as well as a truck. Besides, of all the model types available trucks are the most durable, and they can be used in the park or your garden as well as on a track.

Truck racing is one of the newer classes, with a history dating back only to 1996. Then only electric versions were available, but today there are 2WD electric and nitro stadium trucks, and monster trucks too. Though it remains a developing part of the hobby, nitro trucks are growing in popularity in the UK, predominantly in the Midlands.

With many manufacturers now producing an off-road racing truck, and 4WD models becoming

more popular, the choice is bewildering, so talk to someone who knows and understands the truck world. The most popular trucks raced around the UK come from Team Associated and Team Losi, both US-based companies, though we now also have the Japanese Mugen truck. The Team Associated RC10GT, now in its GT2 guise, has been around for about ten years and its countless ROAR national titles are testament to its bullet-proof mechanics and sublime chassis dynamics.

1:8 Rallycross Buggy – get it dirty

1:8 nitro off-road, or rallycross as it's more commonly known, is currently, without doubt, the largest growth section in RC racing. The BRCA Nationals are seeing full entries, and local clubs are witnessing a steady rise in the number of racers attending each weekend. The number of available cars is likewise at an all time high, but which one is right for you? All are based around the proven competition layout, comprising an aluminium chassis plate to which the three differentials are bolted. Long travel independent suspension arms support the chassis at each corner, and these are controlled by oversize oil-filled shock absorbers. The 3.5cc engine that powers these cars at speeds of up to 50mph is mounted to one side of the chassis, the other side being taken up by the

radio equipment. Different spring-tension rates, damper settings, anti-roll bars settings and adjustable suspension geometry are available to fine tune the handling, and tyres come in various patterns and compounds.

The construction rules laid down by the BRCA limit the fuel tank size to 125cc. This provides sufficient fuel for the five-minute qualifying heats, but fuel stops are necessary for finals, which range from ten to thirty minutes' duration. For this you need to have a good mechanic ready to refuel your car, and the closeness of the racing means some finals are won or lost on the pit stops.

One of the nice things about rallycross racing is that you can buy, off the shelf, exactly the same specification equipment as the top drivers use. This in turn leads to a very level playing field, so that it's the skill of the driver that decides the winner.

1:8 Truggies – massive fun

Not only are 1:8 nitro trucks among the biggest RC models in terms of physical size, but there's also a tremendous range of choice. The racing is good too, as their greater stability and easy-to-drive characteristics make them a lot of fun.

Hot on the successful heels of rallycross buggies come the truggies. The name came about as a combination of 'trucks' and 'buggies' when someone decided to fit big wheels and tyres and a

ABOVE Rallycross is currently the fastest-growing racing class and has benefited enormously from the RTR market, as many kits are ready to be raced just an hour or two after purchase.

The tracks that truggies race on are the same as those for the buggies, with the qualifying and race durations normally the same. Truggies provide a great starting place for people who want to get into nitro off-road racing, as their smoother response and superior stability and handling encourage confidence. But there a number of key differences between a buggy and truggy. The latter is much wider and therefore more stable, while the wheels and tyres are bigger so that grip is better due to their larger footprint. On the power front, instead of the limit being 3.5cc or .21cu as per a rallycross buggy, a truggy can run an engine up to 4.9cc or .30cu and so has even greater power, although its bigger engine will reduce the time on track compared to a smaller one. With that in mind, the rule makers decided that the fuel tank in a truggy could have a capacity as big as 175cc. Despite the option of bigger engines, modern day nitro motors have such immense power that many truggy racers continue to take advantage of the smaller 3.5cc variety and achieve long run-times between refuels thanks to their 175cc tanks.

As a result of all these advantages, truggies will often turn in the fastest laps at a meeting and can be the most exciting to watch.

1:8 Nitro On-Road – fastest of all

Radio control cars come in many different shapes and sizes but with acceleration from zero to 60mph in under two seconds and top speeds in excess of 75mph, is it any wonder that 1:8 nitro on-road is considered the Formula One of RC racing?

ABOVE Using the proven design principles of the 1:8 nitro-powered buggy, the truggy class is booming. Benefits of a truggy include greater stability, a higher level of grip and even better performance in terms of lap times.
(Chris Bates)

truck bodyshell onto a rallycross buggy. Although the first examples were small production run conversions of existing buggies, the rapid growth of the 1:8 nitro off-road sector has ensured that all the leading players in the market now have a truggy kit alongside their buggy.

Most truggies are based around their buggy relatives, which means that many racers find it much easier to compete in both classes by using products from one manufacturer's range, as spares and knowledge of the product can be capitalised upon. That said, many newer truggies are designed specifically for the job, so even though they may appear very similar on the outside their designers have made subtle internal changes so that their performance can be maximised.

RIGHT One-eighth nitro-powered on-road chassis is capable of speeds in excess of 75mph. With this awesome performance from a 3.5cc engine and two-speed gearbox, it's possible to reach 60mph in less than two seconds and drain the fuel tank in under five minutes.

Racing 1:8 on-road (or circuit) will add a whole new meaning to your understanding of the word 'excitement'. Once you've driven a 1:8 car and experienced its awesome power and stunning cornering speed, you'll never be satisfied with driving anything else, and you'll be back for more again and again and again.

A 1:8 scale nitro-powered four-wheel drive car can be built from one of the many available kits, powered by a racing 3.5cc two-stroke engine capable of delivering over 2bhp. Then you and your high-tech scale racing car are just minutes away from the most mind-blowing experience in model car racing. All cars have front and rear independent suspension controlled by fully adjustable shock absorbers and springs. In addition you'll have disc brakes and automatically shifting transmissions, all topped off with a sports car style bodyshell painted in your own individual colour scheme and designed to achieve the very best from your car, both mechanically and aerodynamically.

The 1:8 racing class is a great hobby for the whole family, and besides racing as individuals many father-and-son teams compete in racing events. Once you've got used to the thrill of driving your own car around one of the purpose-built circuits located throughout the country you'll be able to compete in your own first event.

Like most classes, race day generally begins with a practice session in which you'll be able to tune your car and engine for maximum performance. Qualifying rounds last five minutes, but you'll require a pit person to place your car on the track before qualifying begins and to pick it up again at the end. Bear in mind too that once you've qualified for a final you'll have to think about

your race strategy, as you'll need to consider pit stops for refuelling.

Large Scale On-Road – two-stroke on-road racers

Formerly known as quarter scale, large scale caters for 1:5 size machines. The chassis are all based on an aluminium design and they're powered by a 23cc two-stroke engine that runs on petrol-pump unleaded fuel mixed with two-stroke oil.

Large scale circuit racing takes place on outdoor tarmac tracks situated throughout Britain, where the tracks are around 4m to 5m wide and up to 310m long. The engine is limited to a 23cc two-stroke engine (large scale F1 cars are allowed 26cc, and four-wheel-drive up to 30cc). Drive is to the rear wheels only, but can be by cog, chain or shaft, and brakes must be fitted. These come as either discs on the layshaft or outboard discs on the rear wheels or drive shafts. Many have discs all round, usually cable operated but some now use hydraulic.

As a rule even the cheapest kits come complete with everything, apart from radio gear, pre-built and ready to race. They can be upgraded by adding on parts to bring them into line with top-of-the-range cars or to accommodate the wants of the individual driver, by adding adjustable differential and clutches, putting hydraulic brakes all round, or changing to alloy or carbon components. Tyres are moulded rubber (normally fitted with foam inners), with tread patterns and grades of rubber to suit track conditions and drivers' preferences.

The BRCA Large Scale Section runs four classes of saloons: Four-wheel-drive; Eco class for standard kit cars that fall below a set price limit; National class, for all other saloon drivers; and Super National class, made up of the top 12 drivers

ABOVE Size does matter and with a large-scale on-road car you get it all – extra large! Although the car shown here is 2WD (rear-wheel-driven) and weighs around 10kg, it's capable of reaching speeds of over 50mph.

from the previous year's National series in their own premier league. Sports/GT, F1 and Trucks may also be run depending upon entry numbers.

Large scale racing has a growing following, with a very healthy level of competition within the 'travelling circus' of drivers competing in the national Championship. There are also regional championships and ones aimed at the club level driver.

Large Scale Off-Road – big buggies

Using 1:6 scale chassis and two-stroke engines, large scale off-road is one of the most interesting classes, as with their greater size you can enjoy a much better understanding of the mechanics.

Like other scales, 1:6 off-road is spectacular, exciting and lots of fun to take part in. However, unlike the smaller scales these cars have more room inside so can take advantage of the technical advances that their on-road cousins have made over the years. The cars feature hydraulic disc brakes, not only on the front but sometimes on all four corners, and a 26cc two-stroke engine that runs on a mix of unleaded fuel and two-stroke oil. Together with highly sophisticated suspension and drivetrain

technology, the whole package adds up to some pretty amazing racing experiences!

The starting grid is a rainbow of colour, though this soon disappears under a coat of mud or dust! The loose surfaces these cars race on provides a level playing field on which a driver's skill and ability rather than the amount of money spent on his car determine the outcome of a race. Indeed, a completely 'standard' out-of-the-box car can beat one that's been fully modified.

The sight of these 10kg monsters under way is quite awesome! With the cars reaching speeds in excess of 50mph it feels just like scaled down full-size racing.

With more and more large scale off-road clubs appearing you should keep an eye on the BRCA website for further information, and visit your local club if you fancy making the switch to pocket rockets of fun!

1:5 Bikes – two wheels are good

Though they aren't covered in this book – our main concern being four-wheeled models – it's worth bearing in mind that 1:5 RC bikes are also interesting to race. Despite their larger scale, they don't require huge tracks to race on, and success

BELOW With a large 26cc two-stroke engine, not only do these large-scale off-roaders look menacing, but they have a performance to match.

depends more on driver skill and set-up than wallet size.

It's hard to put into words the satisfaction that 1:5 bike racing brings; suffice to say that it's completely different to anything you'll have tried before. The amount of set-up is comparable to any four-wheeled class – ride height affects steering and braking balance, shock oils and spring rates play a huge part in the overall agility of your machine, weight balance vertically as well as horizontally will define the rate of direction change, and so on – but the biggest weapons by far in your arsenal are hand-to-eye co-ordination coupled with an understanding of motorcycle dynamics. Steering a bike is a veritable balance of speed and input, and once it's leaning over a bike demands ultimate attention to carve the correct line. Turn in even more when running wide and you'll understeer off the track. Try to avoid a fallen rider whilst at speed and the bike will tilt slightly rather than jink around the object. The wheels are gyroscopes and contain massive amounts of energy: tilt the wheel left at high speed and the bike steers right, just like the real thing, so remember to flick your steering servo reverse switch before you start!

Larger circuits give a real insight into the sheer speed these machines are capable of, while a smooth driving style and accurate cornering are the key to a hot lap. Tighter circuits really hone your braking and apex accuracy, as well as testing the set-up to the limit.

RC bikes vary in design but follow common construction rules to keep them in scale and a fair representation of the real thing. Some manufacturers supply full kits, even ready-to-run versions of electric and nitro bikes, while specialist companies are developing performance-enhancing packages. The engineering prowess of individuals is also actively encouraged.

In the Superbike formula anything goes within reason – brushed or brushless motors powered by NiMH or LiPo power packs, cable-operated front disc brakes, hydraulic forks with no minimum weight limit, and so on. The same frame or chassis may appear in Superstock, but the 27-turn BRCA stock motor specification and weight limit keep a level playing field to maintain the ultimate competitive spirit. The new brushless 27-turn equivalent Supersport class encompasses everything that's best in Stock racing but opens the door to new brushless technology. The Nitrobike class is only limited by the construction rules, allowing any engine, tank capacity or fuel so long as it fits in the chassis. Anyone appearing on the scene with a standard kit bike is assured a race against someone of equal ability.

Everything else!

The RC racing scene encompasses a multitude of smaller more specialised classes. Some of these have a purely local following while others are incorporated into some of the regional race series. If you're considering an RC car, of any type, our first recommendation would be to find your local club, which will guide you to the best local model shops and provide guidance to the makes they support.

ABOVE RC bikes are cool but are very different to drive (or 'ride') compared to a car or truck. There are specialist shops and websites that will help you get the most from your 1:5 bike. *(Dez Chand)*

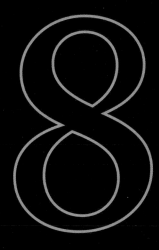

How to design and build a track

Designing a track	**148**
Laying out a track	**150**
Permanent circuits	**153**
Rostrums	**154**
Looking after your track	**155**

Designing a track

The following is offered as a guide to building a temporary on-road racetrack that can be easily packed away, or moved and reused at different locations. This is useful if you intend to race in a sports hall that's used for other things during the week, or if you're putting on a race at a public event or show. By following these simple guidelines you'll have an adaptable track that should last for years.

When designing the track layout, use squared graph paper to draw it out. Make sure that the fast straight sections aren't opposite one another. Ideally the main straight should back on to a series of slower corners to reduce the chance of possible accidents. It's important that the drawing is to scale, as this is the plan that will be used to position the track markers. It's a good idea to have a couple of alternative designs that will still work using the same track markers, as you have to allow for problems at the track location that may prevent you from using your ideal circuit design.

A good basic starting point for a track layout is to have a long main straight leading to a fast sweeping bend that leads into a series of slower corners that eventually lead out to another sweeping bend that joins back up to the straight. If you want to make something a bit more adventurous you can add another straight on the other side of the circuit and then put in a few hairpin bends and chicanes to make it more of a

ABOVE When laying a dirt track you can spray lines where you'd like the track to go, as can clearly be seen in this picture of the DXR team preparing a 1:8 off-road track in a barn.
(CML Distribution)

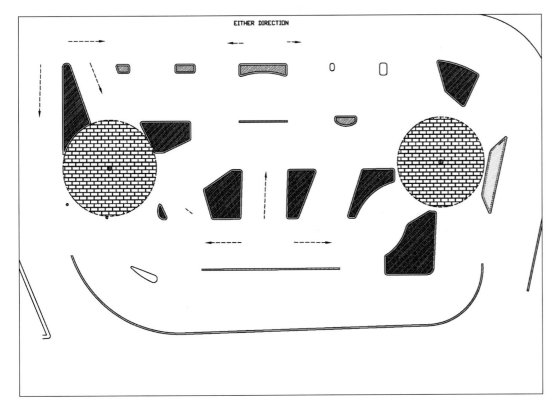

LEFT This digital format diagram of the 1:10 off-road Kidderminster Model Car Club track shows its permanent features. The shaded areas are the infield, with the circular areas being block paving. The arrows indicate any changes in elevation. *(Paul Worsley)*

challenge. Just remember to make sure the track is wide enough for at least a couple of cars to drive side-by-side at every point and don't make the circuit too twisty and technical so that it just causes lots of crashes. What you need to aim for is a track that's fast and fun to drive, but also demanding enough to test the racers' driving skills.

Track markers

Before the event you'll have to prepare the track markers. Commercial prefabricated track markers are available, but these can be expensive and may limit the number of different track designs you can use. An alternative is to make your own, which is what many clubs that race at various venues

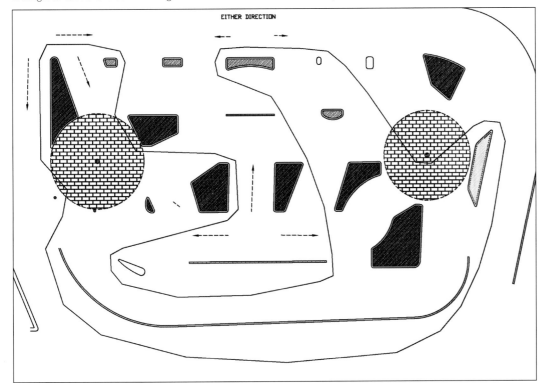

LEFT With multiple layouts, the continuous line shows the one that was chosen for the National event in 2007. The rostrum position is at the bottom, with the straight in front, although the diagram indicates that the racing line may be curved for the best corner speeds. *(Paul Worsley)*

straight piping to secure this to the carpet in the same way.

To make the corners as high or deep as the pipe being used to mark out the rest of the track you can sandwich wooden blocks between two discs. You can use one corner marker to denote a tight corner or hairpin, or several together to mark out a longer more sweeping curve.

Where the straight markers run up to the corner pieces you'll need to join them with flexible white PVC strips cut to the same width as the pipe. Attach a wooden block, of the same size as you've used to join the straight pipes together, to each end of the PVC strips. Then push these blocks into each open end of the straight pipes that run up to the corner. This should provide a nice smooth finish to the corners and make the whole track look very professional.

If you want to save money, or don't have time to make track markers, a simple alternative is to use lengths of rope or sand-filled fire hoses. Both offer a useful alternative to downpipe, but neither will look quite as good. Suitable heavyweight rope is available from a number of sources, such as boat chandlers, and can be attached to your MDF corner discs by simply placing a screw through the rope and into the disc.

Corners can also be marked using simple football training discs, which can be easily obtained from any sports shop for as little as under £10 for 50 discs. These have the advantage of enabling a car to 'clip' them without causing it to spin or incur any damage. For off-road cars, they can be placed underneath a carpet or taped in position to provide a series of 'mogul' bumps to test the cars' suspensions and the drivers' skills.

Laying out a track

When you arrive at the track location, and before laying out your track, survey the area carefully. Make sure it's flat and that there are no drain covers or bumps in the floor that are likely to affect the

ABOVE Green carpet is used on the infield to increase the track's definition, whilst the white track markings provide a good contrast against the grey carpet.

around the country do. These are usually made up from white square-section guttering downpipe, as it's strong and kind to model cars – they usually bounce off it in a collision with little or no damage. The straight downpipe is joined together using wooden blocks that are just the right size to fit inside. These are pushed into one end of each section of pipe, leaving enough sticking out so that the open end of another piece of pipe can be slid over it, thus joining the two pieces together. These are then secured by driving screws through the pipe and into the wooden blocks inside.

The pipe is fine for the straight parts of the track, and it's also good for marking the edge of the circuit, but you'll also need a way to mark the corners. The best way to make corner markers is to cut discs from a sheet of medium density fibreboard (MDF) – a good material to work with as it's easy to shape with power tools and to paint after sealing. These discs are substantial enough to remain in position even if they're hit by fast-moving cars, but are light enough to be portable if you need to store the track away. You can ensure that they stay in place by putting some self-adhesive hook-and-loop fastener on the bottom – just use the hook half, as this will stick to the felt carpet. Attach some more to the underneath of the

BELOW The UK hosted the on-road World Championships in 1998 and created this awesome track using the proven system of square downpipe and MDF wooden corners.

LEFT The Maritime Racing track is laid out on carpet with the edges taped together.

cars, as even small bumps or imperfections can have a big effect on cars when they're racing at speed.

Once you're happy with the surface it's time to lay out the track. If you've opted for carpet (see below) this can now be rolled out and laid in strips. It's important that the carpet is laid out straight and level and without any ripples. Each strip must be carefully lined up with the rest so that there are no gaps between them. The carpet is then carefully taped together along the joins using carpet, masking or duct tape.

When the whole track area has been carpeted you can mark off the edges using some of the downpipe. Then it's time to lay out the circuit. Following your scale plan, lay each piece out where it should go and make sure the whole circuit works

before joining anything together. Once it's all down and you're happy with it give it a test-run. This will give you a chance to see if the track flows properly, if the corners are in the right places, and if it's wide enough everywhere. Make any necessary adjustments and then you're ready to race. For added effect you should consider laying some green carpet on the infield sections, which will make the whole circuit look more professional.

Indoor track material

While it's possible to race on the wooden floors typically found in sports halls, this surface tends to be quite slippery and requires special tyres to get the best grip. This is why many temporary indoor tracks tend to be laid out using a special grey-coloured felt carpet. As well as providing good grip

FAR LEFT Specialist track markers are available, such as this RoadRail system that locks together.

LEFT As with most methods of track marking, the RoadRail system has advantages and disadvantages. Although it's easy to lay out, its barrier properties aren't as good as the gutter system.

place either by double-sided tape on the underside or by being stuck together in strips by means of masking tape.

Off-road alternative

The easiest way to build a model car track is just to find a large open piece of grass or tarmac and lay it out on that. This will only work for cars designed to race outside, and is particularly well suited to off-road buggies, but it's simple and easy. Track markers range from traffic cones or old rope to sand-filled fire hoses or flexible drainpipe. The same rules follow when laying a track outside as inside: try and design your circuit layout on some graph paper first so you know what you want it to look like – it makes everything a bit easier when you get to your track site and enables you to get the circuit laid out faster, giving you more time to race and enjoy it.

If you do intend to race in a field or car park, don't forget to ask the owner's permission first. If they don't like the sound of the idea at first you may be able to talk them round by explaining that you only intend to have some fun and agreeing to clear up after you. It's much nicer to do it this way than to get thrown out of somewhere without having the chance to explain.

If you're considering building an off-road track it's

ABOVE On a grass track you can use flexible hose for track marking, with a long peg or nail through the middle to fix it down. As the pipe isn't rigid it's kind on the cars too.

for most types of model car tyres, both foam and rubber, it's easy to put down, take up and store, and looks good when it's in use.

The carpet that most clubs use is referred to as Primafelt and is available from www.primadirect.co.uk. It was developed exclusively for RC racing and benefits from being a very low pile, hard-wearing, flame retardant fabric that offers minimal friction. It can be secured in

well worth thinking about a few aspects prior to designing it. First of all, an off-road track will often feature a number of jumps, bumps and berms that have to be easily seen from the rostrum. Therefore many 1:10 off-road tracks have the main straight at the far side, as this is the easiest section of track to negotiate, which means that the more challenging areas can be positioned closer to or in front of the rostrum. That said, this can't happen in nitro classes because of the pit lane – this section of the track has to be under the rostrum, and therefore so does the main straight that runs parallel. If you had the pit lane anywhere else it would be difficult to arrive at a layout where it could be easily accessed when leaving or rejoining the track. Also, you have to consider that when you pit for repairs or refuelling you lose time, and this is why the pit lane is next to the fastest part of a race track.

Marshalling

This is a requirement of any track and the positioning of the marshals should therefore be considered during the design stage. There would be little point in designing a layout where it's unsafe for a marshal to stand on the track due to the incline of a bank or a series of jumps that sends cars high into the air. To make marshalling easier and help provide drivers with a clearer view it's a good idea to place crates on the infield so that the marshals can sit down, thereby obscuring less of the track.

You should have your marshal points clearly identified by means of a cone, for example, or a numbered board. This means that you can move or rotate the points should the number of drivers in a heat or final change. Also, some clubs ask their marshals to wear a fluorescent jacket or bib so that they can be clearly seen and identified.

Permanent circuits

There are a number of permanent on- and off-road racing venues around the country. On-road tarmac tracks look like miniature versions of their full size counterparts, with painted grid markings and built-up kerbing. Permanent off-road circuits tend to offer good facilities for competitors and feature different track surfaces to make them a bit more interesting than just grass. The best way to find your nearest permanent racing facility is to either ask at your local model shop or visit the British Radio Car Association website at www.brca.org, which will have a list of clubs in your area. Then you can contact them to find out what type of track they have.

BELOW The KO Raceway in West London is one of the best-prepared on-road tracks in the UK. *(www.wlrc.co.uk)*

ABOVE Benches are perfect to give you just enough elevation to improve your view.

ABOVE RIGHT Many clubs race in school halls and utilise the staging at one end of the building. *(Jon Painter)*

BELOW The Oswestry club made use of a curtain-sided trailer for their National events in 2006 and 2007. As you can see, there's lots of space and the drivers are protected too.

BELOW RIGHT Scaffolding makes a great temporary rostrum. This one was used at a promotional race meeting at the Sandown racecourse in Surrey.

Rostrums

Once you have a track, you may wish to consider building or getting hold of something to serve as a rostrum. Rostrums may be either temporary or permanent, using something to hand or requiring specialist equipment. If you're racing indoors you may have access to benches that can be carefully stacked against a wall to provide elevation. These should obviously be secured to ensure the drivers' safety when they're stood on.

Some halls may have staging at one end that can be used. Remember that you only need to raise the driving position by a couple of feet to see the whole track. The staging is often a good way of achieving this as it's safe, not too high, and reduces the amount of work you have to do before and after a race meeting.

Temporary outdoor rostrums

Naturally, if you're outdoors rostrums aren't as easy to make, and as the tracks are often much larger you'll need greater elevation. One popular method used by clubs is to get hold of a 'curtain-sided' trailer. These are essentially the back half of an articulated lorry but they provide ample space, have a safety rail built in, and offer some shelter from inclement weather.

The second and more popular alternative is to make a temporary rostrum using scaffolding and boards. Not only are these materials much more readily available, but you can tweak and refine the design to personalise it to the track or the situation. Making it longer or higher is easy if you have the parts, and a scaffolding design can be stripped down and packed away into a relatively small area for storage. You will, of course, need some boards to serve as a platform, as well as steps or treads so that you can access the driving area.

Going permanent

Should you wish to make your rostrum a permanent feature, there's lots of choice when considering what approach to take. For instance, you can include a portable 'building' underneath the rostrum as a base for the event organisers. This obviously gives the rostrum the necessary height as well as providing the security of a solid, sturdy base. Building a rostrum out of bricks or blocks may require foundations as well as permission from the local Council, so a lot of the time rostrums are made out of wood. That said, if you have a scaffolding system already in place a simple way to improve its looks is to clad it in wood and decorate it in the club colours. Maybe the most elaborate rostrum-come-race-control

building in the UK is that at the CML Raceway in Berkshire, which utilises an open-top double-decker bus!

Looking after your track

Once a track has been laid, bear in mind that it may require some work to maintain it. Although a tarmac on-road track may seem the perfect surface, as there's no grass to cut, there's a chance that the grip will be low, but you can improve this by adding various solutions. An old but trusted method is to 'Coke' it, meaning you spray carbonated or fizzy drink onto the surface. This makes the track sticky and helps the cars to grip. A variant called 'sugar watering' involves spraying it with a citrus drink such as grape juice or orange juice. Racers will often refer to a track as being 'green' when there's no grip. Soft racing tyres, whether foam or rubber, will start to engrain into the surface of a 'green' track – which is good in the dry, but when it gets wet the 'rubbered in' sections can be like driving on ice!

With an off-road dirt track things may be a little harder. Some have to be regularly watered to help provide grip whereas others may need to be swept to remove loose dirt on the surface that otherwise acts like marbles. With a dirt track and soft tyres you'll often find that the rubber will eventually get into the top surface and the racing line will change colour. This is what we call a 'blue groove', and the traction can be amazing in this situation.

Many off-road tracks in the UK run on a predominantly grass surface, which is regularly mown short to maintain it and prevent weed growth. However, the power and grip of RC cars leads to the track surface deteriorating quickly – even during a single meeting. The landing points after jumps often become rutted and broken up as cars' bumpers dig into the surface when they land

incorrectly, and the corner apexes rapidly become devoid of their grass surface as tyres scrabble for grip and wheelspin under acceleration.

When racing on a temporary track this problem can be managed by simply changing the layout so as to rest worn areas and allow the grass to grow back, but on permanent tracks it can be more of a headache. Many permanent tracks are composed of a number of 'islands' that can be linked by hosing or flexible piping to create different track layouts. This partly overcomes the problem and allows for certain areas to be rested, but if the problem is on a common corner or jump then the only real answer is to use a more durable material for the racing surface.

Astroturf is one solution and is favoured by many clubs in the UK, as it can enable year-round racing. When laying the Astroturf, though, some groundwork preparation may be in order so as to avoid weed growth, and careful consideration needs to be given to where to start and finish the sections. For instance, it may be advisable to start an Astroturf section a little way before a corner so as to avoid its edges becoming a hazard to cars in the braking zone.

Alternatively, some clubs lay tarmac or block paving on certain corners, which really tests the drivers' skills and set-ups. Negotiating a change in grip level for one corner can be the undoing of many promising drives as a car will behave quite differently on different surfaces. That said, it becomes a truly satisfying experience when the corner is driven fast and successfully, as an immediate advantage can often be gained.

In the past some clubs have successfully used open meshing and nets in the grass and soil substructure to help prevent the top surface from deteriorating too much, but one of the greatest challenges in off-road racing is being able to read the differences in tracks as they develop during a meeting. This makes off-road racing unique, as often the drivers will have to find a different line to negotiate a bump that develops as the day progresses.

ABOVE LEFT You can clad the scaffolding in wood to make it look very professional.

ABOVE By soaking the track with certain liquids you can increase the grip it offers. Here a team 'sugar waters' the World Championship track in South Africa.

BELOW At the World Championships in Florida they regularly watered the surface to get the track into the best condition.

Appendix 1 – Glossary

Like any sport or hobby, radio control car racing uses a whole host of technical phrases that you need to learn. This guide will help you understand some of the more commonly used jargon of the RC world.

2WD – This abbreviation describes a car with two-wheel-drive, and in most cases the two wheels are the ones on the rear axle. One-tenth scale off-road buggies come in either 2WD or 4WD platforms. Two-wheel-drive cars are harder to drive than their 4WD relations but are simpler to build and maintain.

4WD – Four-wheel-drive cars have all four wheels receiving power, which gives them greater grip and makes them easier to drive. One-tenth scale off-

RIGHT This 4WD buggy from JConcepts features a transmission that powers all four wheels for greater performance.

road buggies come in either 2WD or 4WD platforms.

A final – The final race of the day, populated by the best drivers at a meeting, These may have set the fastest times or have been the most consistent at the meeting during qualifying. The winner of the A final is the overall winner of the race meeting, and at large events can take home a trophy or plaque to signify their achievement.

ABS – Anti-lock braking systems are built into the speed control of electric cars and some of the more elaborate transmitter units of nitro-powered models. In order to prevent the brakes from locking, the transmitter pulses the servo very quickly under braking, just like some of the systems adopted by full-size car manufacturers. See page 114.

Ackermann – Named after its inventor, the 'Ackermann angle' is the relationship of the inside wheel compared to the outside when the steering is on full lock. 'More Ackermann' is where the inside wheel is at a greater angle (more lock) than the outer one. Ackermann helps to make a car turn and is often adjustable by moving part of the steering linkage.

Additive – A special liquid used to soften the surface of both rubber and foam tyres to increase the amount of grip they generate.

After-run oil – After finishing with their engine for the day, nitro owners put after-run oil into it to help prevent corrosion and give its internal parts a protective coating.

Air filter – As its name suggests, an air filter cleans the air before it enters the engine via the carburettor. The filter is soaked in filter oil, which improves its filtering qualities, and should be cleaned and re-oiled at regular intervals to maintain performance. If an air filter isn't oiled or, in extreme circumstances, isn't even fitted it's possible to wear an engine out in a matter of minutes, as fine dust simply destroys the internal components.

Anodised – Although this process actually hardens the exterior surface of a metal part, most people believe anodising to be no more than a way of changing its colour. Though many different colours are available a lot of manufacturers stick to just one, to identify their parts from others'.

Anti-roll bar – This is normally a small metal bar mounted from one side of the car's suspension to the other, with the bar held in the middle to act as a fixing point. An anti-roll bar allows the wheels to retain independent movement, but when one wheel goes up added pressure is placed upon the bar and stiffens the action of the wheel on the other side. If the wheels go up together, the anti-roll bar has no effect. Fitting an anti-roll bar to the rear of the car can help to prevent it pushing wide in the corners.

ABOVE An anti-roll bar stops the chassis rolling in a corner without affecting the suspension's bump-absorbing properties.

Anti-squat – This is the angle at which the rear wishbones sit when viewed from the side. As the name suggests, anti-squat prevents the rear suspension from squatting under acceleration and can be used as a tuning aid to improve the car's performance under acceleration or over bumps. Most cars use between 1° and 3° of anti-squat, although you can run at zero in extreme circumstances.

Armature – The central part of a motor that rotates inside the can. The armature's shaft extends at both ends, more notably at the non-endbell end where there's a flat part for the pinion to attach to. Coils of wire are wrapped around the armature's stack to produce a magnetic field that opposes the one produced by the two magnets in the can.

B and C finals – Drivers who don't make the A final are classified in lower finals. Usually an A final is made up of the top ten drivers, and in such instances drivers from 11 to 20 go into the B final, drivers 21 to 30 go into the C final, and so on.

Backmarker – A slow-moving car that's being lapped by the leaders is referred to as being a backmarker. Race officials will always ask the driver of a backmarker to act courteously and move out of the way of faster cars.

Battery capacity – The capacity of a pack of batteries is determined by the mAh (milliamp-hour) figure on the side of a single cell. The latest batteries on the market have around 4,200 to 4,300mAh.

Battery pack – This refers to the pack of cells fitted to an electric car that provides power to the motor. The higher the capacity (mAh) the longer the car will run for but the more expensive they are to purchase. Entry-level battery packs are generally supplied in stick pack format, usually with an industry-standard connector that links the battery to the speed control.

RIGHT Metal bearings are much more efficient than a bronze or plastic bushing. This bearing features a rubber shield for protection.

FAR RIGHT An example of a brushless package from LRP Electronic.

Bearing – Often called a ball race, a bearing is made of metal and is fitted in areas such as the hubs and gearboxes where there are rotating parts. Inside the inner and outer races are very small balls which allow the inner surface to move whilst the other one stays in a fixed position. A bearing is a much better alternative than a bushing. It has less friction, works more smoothly and reduces wear. Bearings need to be lubricated with suitable oil and grease to prevent wear and heat build-up. If mistreated a bearing can lock and cause premature component wear and poor handling.

Berm – A banked bend that's usually found on an off-road track. This term is also used in BMX racing.

Body posts – These are moulded plastic posts that are screwed to the chassis of the car to support the bodyshell. Usually there are four posts (sometimes five), with one at each corner. As there's a massive range of bodyshells available the height of the posts is adjustable so that you can raise or lower the position of the body.

Bottoming out – A chassis is said to 'bottom out' when it hits the ground, either at the front or rear or both. This can be caused by either the ride height being too low or by poor suspension settings. Off-road cars can bottom out regularly off large jumps and this is more acceptable than in on-road racing, in which bottoming out is a sign of bad set-up and if the chassis scrapes the ground it'll have a detrimental effect on the handling.

BRCA – The British Radio Car Association is the official governing body for RC racing in the UK. Joining the BRCA entitles the licence holder to insurance cover and other benefits. A BRCA licence is required to compete at sanctioned events in the UK.

Brush wear – The brushes on an electric motor will wear during use, and after a period of time will require replacing. If conditions are very wet brush wear is accelerated and you should protect the motor against water impregnation. Soft brushes wear faster than harder ones, although you can affect the wear rate by the tension of the brush spring. Different combinations can be used as a means of tuning motor performance to the track and conditions.

Brushes – Fitted to an electric motor, brushes are used to transmit electrical current from the speed control's wires through to the commutator. They're held in place by metal guides on one end of the motor and are pushed up against the surface of the commutator by special springs. A range of different compounds of brush can be used to change the motor's power output and performance.

Brushless – A type of motor that, due to its design, doesn't require brushes in order to work. Brushless motors are much more complex than their brushed counterparts in the way that they work, but due to their design they demand less maintenance. There are two types – sensored and sensorless. The former utilises a sensor lead that connects from the motor to the speed controller and tells the latter the position of the armature inside the motor can. A sensorless system doesn't need this lead and is less common, especially in racing.

Buggy – A popular general term used to describe 1:10 off-road cars available in either 2WD or 4WD formats. They can race on specialist tracks that incorporate a number of surfaces including grass, dirt, Astroturf, concrete and tarmac, or a mixture of them all.

Bump steer – When the toe angle changes as the suspension moves up and down it's described as 'bump steer'. Normally this only occurs on the front wheels but in some cases it can happen on the rear suspension. Bump steer isn't necessarily a bad thing and it can be used as a tuning aid, although most racers try and set their chassis without it. It can be altered by raising or lowering one end of the pivot point on the steering linkage that connects the hub to the inner steering rack or bell crank.

Bushing – A simple alternative to a metal bearing, often found on entry-level specification models or in places where it's impossible to fit a bearing. A bushing is much cheaper to make and is usually constructed from a soft material such as bronze or plastic. Replacing these early on will reduce wear and increase performance as well as offering better reliability.

FAR LEFT It's possible to purchase specialist glue designed for gluing tyres on.

LEFT This centrifugal clutch is a four-shoe competition item and uses a combination of alloy (blue) and plastic shoes. You can tune it by changing the spring tension.

CA – Cyanoacrylate is the technical name for the solution we know as superglue. It's used to hold rubber tyres to their rims and for other small jobs, as it's easy to use and dries quickly.

Camber – When viewed from the front of the car, camber is the angle between vertical and a line passing down through the middle of the wheel, parallel to the wheel hub. The camber is said to be negative when the top of the wheel leans in towards to the car, positive when the top of the wheel leans out. The camber angle will change during cornering due to the movement of the chassis on the suspension. Most radio control touring cars will use a negative camber angle of around 2° on the front wheels to give good tyre contact in the corners.

Can – The steel tin-can-shaped part of an electric motor into which the magnets are fixed. The armature slots into a bearing in one end of the can, and into the motor endbell at the other.

Carbon fibre – A modern composite material that's both light and stiff. It's found on competition models and is used to limit flex and aid set-up.

Carburettor – The carburettor or 'carb' fitted to an engine mixes the fuel and air. It's adjusted to ensure that the correct proportions of air and fuel are used to create a flammable mixture that, when drawn into the engine's combustion chamber, will ignite to create power.

Caster – When viewed from the side of the car, caster is the angle between vertical and a line drawn through the upper and lower outboard suspension pivot points. At the front of the car, the upper pivot is always slightly behind the lower one, creating a self-aligning force that helps to pull the front wheels back into the 'straight-ahead' position when exiting a bend. Caster needs to be set the same on both sides of the car.

Channels – This term is used to describe the number of RC control operations. For example, most radio control cars require two channels – one for the steering and a second for the throttle and brakes. More expensive radio equipment can have a greater number of channels, which can be used,

for example, for changing between forward and reverse gear on a nitro car.

Chunking – Foam racing tyres 'chunk' when a lump of the foam is ripped out, often as a result of colliding with another car or a track marker.

Clipping point – The apex of a corner, usually indicated on the track by a coloured marker. The racing line through a corner involves aiming for the apex or clipping point.

Clutch – Just like on a full-size car, the clutch transmits the engine power to the wheels in a nitro-powered RC car. Most clutches can be adjusted by the driver to alter the engagement point, or biting point, of the clutch, to suit the conditions or engine power.

Comm lathe – A small purpose-built lathe used to skim a thin layer of copper from the electric motor commutator. For an electric motor to operate efficiently it's important to ensure good contact between the brushes and the commutator. The best method is to regularly fit new brushes and skim a clean surface on the commutator.

Commutator – This is the copper part of the armature located at one end of an electric motor. The motor's brushes sit against the commutator to conduct the power around the coils wrapped around the armature.

Crankcase – The main aluminium case of a nitro engine, into which all of the components fit. Many crankcases have small cooling fins built into them to help ensure that the engine doesn't get too hot.

Crankshaft – The part of a nitro engine that converts the reciprocating movement of the piston moving up and down in the cylinder into a rotary motion. The clutch bolts onto the end of the crankshaft.

Crystals – Crystals come as a matching pair; one goes in the transmitter, the other in the receiver. They determine the specific radio frequency the car will operate on. This must not clash with the frequencies assigned to other cars in a race.

CVD – Short for 'constant velocity driveshaft', the type of driveshaft fitted to most four-wheel-drive competition cars. The pivot ball design aims to minimise power loss while still allowing free movement in all directions so that the suspension can function.

Dampers – Another name for the shock absorbers. Dampers have the task of keeping all four wheels on the ground at all times, giving the tyres their best chance to grip. The dampers on a model car can be highly tuneable, with different springs, oil, pistons, limiters and mounting points available to change the handling characteristics. Soft dampers make the car less responsive but more forgiving to drive. See also 'shock absorbers'.

Decals – A term often used to describe stickers. Some decals can be applied using water to help position them, but most are adhesive-backed for simplicity.

Deck – A term used to refer to a level of the chassis, as in the top deck (upper level) or chassis deck (lower level).

Dialled – An American term used to describe a well-balanced car that handles excellently.

Differential – A differential or 'diff' allows one wheel to rotate at a different speed to the other, which means that when a car's cornering it helps it to maintain speed through the turn. Essentially there are two versions of differential, a ball-type and a gear-type. The former uses a circle of small ball bearings held between two metal rings; a screw through the middle adjusts the pressure applied, which in turn alters the action of the differential – this can then be used as a tuning aid. Gear-type differentials aren't externally adjustable but rely on a lubricant, either grease or silicon oil, to control the speed of internal components. Gear-type diffs are generally more robust than ball-type, with the latter requiring more maintenance.

Discharge tray – These trays or discharge boards, as they're often referred to, allow you to discharge any remaining power from your battery pack at the end of a race. Unlike a normal discharger, the tray discharges the cells individually, which offers better conditioning of the cell than discharging the pack as a whole. The tray has one resistor for each cell and the pack clips into place. Usually an LED will indicate the status of each cell.

Dog-bone – As the name suggests, this is a driveshaft that looks like a dog bone. They're usually fitted to introductory specification kits due to their simplicity and strength. Most manufacturers will offer upgrades for dog-bones in the form of a universal joint (UJ) or constant velocity (CVD) driveshaft.

Double-sided tape – As the name suggests, unlike regular tape that's only sticky on one side this padded material is sticky on both sides, and is used to secure electrical components in a car. Though it's used principally in electric-powered cars it also secures the receiver and speed control in nitro models.

Downforce – An invisible effect that occurs when air hits the bodyshell or the wing on a car. Increasing the level of downforce will offer better control in corners but will slow the car down on the straights due to the increase in drag.

DP or diametrical pitch – This technical phrase relates to the profile of the spur gear teeth. Most classes adopt a standard diametrical pitch, for example 1:10 electric models generally use 48dp while 1:12 use 64dp. The smaller the number, the more open and aggressive the profile, with less teeth used over the same distance.

Drifting – One of the most recent classes in RC, drifting is all about control and style rather than speed around the track. Hailing from the US and Japan, it's developed from a form of full-size competition that's growing in popularity around the world. Marks are awarded to the drivers who demonstrate the smoothest slides, the best control and the longest drifts through a corner. See page 107.

Droop – This is the amount of down travel that the suspension has to offer. You generally run more droop on tracks with large jumps or bumpy surfaces, as this provides greater shock movement to handle such demands.

EFRA – The European Federation of Radio Automobiles is the European governing body for RC car racing. It sets the rules and the race

RIGHT A differential allows the inside wheel to turn at a lower speed than the outside one. This example uses gears inside and is oil-filled for lubrication.

FAR RIGHT Drifting is one of the latest RC classes to hit the UK. This Yokomo kit is based on a full-size car raced in Japan.

calendar for the European Championships and other prestigious events.

Electronic speed control – Often referred to as an ESC or simply 'the speedo', this invaluable component translates your input from the transmitter into the amount of power put through to the motor. Modern-day speed controls are very complex and technical and offer different profiles to alter the torque curves as well as adjustable braking levels and programs to suit different tracks and conditions. See page 52.

EMF – This is generated by a motor during braking and is a potential source of interference and accentuated arcing that causes wear to the commutator.

Endbell – This is the end of the motor that contains all the important elements, such as the brushes, springs and soldering tags. On more powerful and expensive motors the endbell can be removed to make changes to the set-up as well as allow the armature to be removed from the motor can for maintenance.

EPA – End-point adjustment, a transmitter feature that allows you to ensure the servos move to their maximum position without straining, which can cause damage. See page 114.

FET servo – A FET servo offers better performance than a standard unit and in an electric chassis is used for the steering, to increase the reaction time from the driver's input to the effect at the wheels. These high-torque, high-speed units may require more power from the battery but they're easily able to handle the demands of the latest trucks with large, heavy wheels.

Frequency – A transmitter operates on a changeable frequency that's used to send signals to the receiver. The frequencies allowed for use with model cars are approved by the Government and can differ from country to country. In the UK, only specific frequencies on the 27MHz, 40MHz and 2.4GHz bands are allowed.

FTD – This stands for 'fastest time of the day' and refers to a qualifying system where the driver who completes the most laps in the allotted race time takes pole position for the A final. At the end of qualifying the drivers are sorted into order with the fastest at the top, based on their best single performance. The drivers who completed the most laps go into the A final.

Glitch – A term used to describe momentary loss of radio contact with the car. There can be a variety of different causes, but unreliable electrical connections, a broken receiver aerial or insufficient suppression of the electric motor are common. Sometimes a change of frequency can provide a cure, particularly if the new frequency is spaced further apart from the other cars in the race. Severe glitches are usually called radio interference.

Glow plug – A device that's used to start and keep a nitro engine running. A battery inside the glow plug heats up a tiny platinum alloy wire to create enough heat to make the end of the coil glow. This then ignites the fuel/air mixture inside the engine when it's turned over. Once the engine is up to temperature the battery can be removed, the heat generated by the compression being sufficient to keep the glow plug hot enough to continue igniting the mixture. A bad glow plug will often cause an engine to run erratically or stop.

Gurney – Named after the person who came up with the principle, the Gurney, or Gurney flap, is a vertical section of a wing that increases downforce but also creates more drag.

Heatsink – A finned piece of aluminium that's connected to motors, nitro engines or speed controls. The mass of material of the heatsink

FAR LEFT A speed control is a tiny piece of electrical equipment that converts the throttle inputs from your transmitter to the electric motor.

FAR LEFT A FET servo offers high performance in terms of speed and torque.

LEFT Although it looks simple, a glow plug is vital in ensuring that an engine works correctly.

RIGHT The heatsink
shown here is fitted to
the top of a speed
control to draw heat
away from the internal
components.

FAR RIGHT Some
moulded foam inserts
as used in touring
car racing.

draws heat away from the item and allows it to
run cooler.

Hooked up – American slang for a car getting
good traction.

Hop-ups – Upgrade parts or aftermarket
accessories that improve the look or performance
of your RC model.

IFMAR – The International Federation of Model
Auto Racing sanctions the official World
Championship events for the major model car
classes. The venue for the event is usually
alternated between EFRA (Europe), FEMCA (the Far
East), FAMAR (South America/South Africa) and
ROAR (North America).

Inserts – Made of either foam or sponge, an insert
is doughnut shaped and is placed inside moulded
rubber tyres to provide a firmer feel and ensure that
the tyre retains its shape. The shape, material,
firmness and dimensions of the insert can be used
to alter the characteristics of a tyre.

Internal combustion – A type of engine used in
radio control cars, 'IC' or internal combustion
referring to its method of producing power. Many
people refer to a model that features an IC engine
as a 'nitro' or 'gas' kit.

Kick-up – The angle at which the suspension
arms are mounted at the front of a car. Kick-up can
be adjusted by changing the suspension arm
mounts or another part of the chassis. Generally
more kick-up helps on bumpy surfaces whereas
less kick-up gives a more aggressive feeling to
the steering.

Lapping – Term used when a car has gained a
whole lap over a slower car and is about to
overtake it. When being lapped, it's good manners
to drive wide round a corner and let the faster car
by, especially during qualifying.

Large-scale – The biggest RC cars, ranging from
1:4 through to 1:6 scale. Due to their huge size,
large-scale kits are powered by bigger two-stroke
22cc engines that use regular unleaded fuel mixed
with oil. These impressive models also require large
areas to race on and possess different
characteristics to smaller kits, such as mechanical
brakes on the front and rear axles and other
innovative features.

Lean – A situation where the carburettor on a nitro
engine is being supplied with less fuel than it
needs. Running an engine a little lean will improve
the fuel economy but can cause the engine to get
too hot. Continuous lean running will cause
premature failure and speed up the wear rate of the
engine. When an engine is over lean it will regularly
stop and become erratic in its performance.

Lexan – Technically referred to as polycarbonate,
Lexan is the plastic material used to make
bodyshells. In its pure form, the transparent,
colourless Lexan is placed over a mould to create
its shape. Lexan bodies are painted on the inside
so that the paint is protected from scratching and
flaking. Many modern-day RTR kits come with 'pre-
painted' bodies that are actually moulded using a
pre-coloured or multi-coloured sheet of Lexan.

LiPo – Lithium Polymer are the latest type of RC
battery cells, and can be used in transmitters as
well as for powering cars. They offer a number of
benefits, including high voltage and high capacity,
but are extremely fragile to use and require a LiPo-
compatible charger.

Loop – The part of an RC racetrack that registers
transponder signals as cars pass over it, to count
the laps and measure lap times.

Magnets – Most modern-day electric motors feature
a pair of magnets inside the motor can that create a
magnetic field. This field is opposed by the magnetic
field generated by the coils of wire on the armature.

RIGHT Lexan or
polycarbonate is used
to make bodyshells, as
it's strong as well
as flexible.

FAR LEFT The mesh is the relationship between two gears.

LEFT A nitro-powered kit in action.

Matching – A process used by battery specialists to cycle individual cells to determine key elements such as overall capacity, voltage and resistance. By selecting a pack using cells that are as similar as possible, the performance is improved over that of a pack of random cells.

Mesh – The relationship between two interlinked gears, usually the spur and pinion on an electric car or the main gear and clutch bell on a nitro-powered model. If you set the mesh too tight it can affect power and make the components operate hot due to the friction. Set the mesh too loose and you run the risk of damaging the gears. Generally a perfect mesh will also run a lot quieter than one that's too tight or too loose, as this can be rather noisy. A neat trick to setting the mesh is to feed a piece of paper between the pinion and spur gear. Press the gears together and then tighten the screws. Roll the gears and the paper can be removed, leaving a perfect mesh.

Micro car – A very small scale of RC car that ranges from 1:18 to 1:24. Cars of this size can be raced indoors at home and are often sold ready-built and complete with a radio transmitter.

MMPR – Millimetres per revolution. See page 103.

Model memory – A feature in some transmitters that allows different settings to be programmed and stored for different cars. See page 115.

Modified motor – Modified motors come in a range of designs and performance ratings. The racing class allows any modified motor to be used, whereas other classes are limited to a single specification motor in order to control performance and costs.

Mogul – A type of bump on an off-road track, similar to those encountered in skiing. Moguls require skill both when setting the car's suspension, in order to absorb some of the bump energy, and in choosing a driving line that minimises the risk of the car becoming unsettled or crashing.

Monster truck – One of the most popular categories of RC at the moment. Though monster trucks can also be powered by either batteries or an electric motor, the most common examples are nitro-powered. The trucks are either 1:10 or 1:8 scale and feature huge wheels and tyres, massive ground clearance and long travel suspension. That said, there are some micro scale monster trucks for use indoors which retain the principle of ground clearance and large rubber tyres.

NiCD – Nickel Cadmium.

NiMH – Nickel-Metal Hydride.

Nitro – A kit that uses an internal combustion (IC) engine rather than an electric motor. The term comes from the small quantities of nitro-methane that are added to the specially blended fuel that's used. This comes in a range of types. The bigger engines will operate with a greater percentage of nitro in the fuel, the most common proportions being 10 per cent for a .12ci size engine through to 30 per cent for a .21ci or .30ci engine. Changing nitro fuel types or manufacturers will require the engine to be adjusted accordingly.

One-way – This device allows the front wheels of a four-wheel-drive car to freewheel off power but then transmits the drive to all four wheels again under acceleration. It's installed either as a replacement for a front differential or on the centre layshaft. Using a one-way increases the amount of steering off-power, but under braking only the rear wheels are slowed down so you have to apply the brakes in a controlled manner to avoid the rear sliding or spinning out. In off-road, some drivers will use this characteristic to help negotiate corners.

Oversteer – This occurs when the rear of a car loses traction and slides, making the vehicle turn

LEFT This 4WD buggy is displaying signs of oversteer, indicated by the body roll and opposite lock being applied.
(www.oople.com)

harder than expected. To avoid oversteer, you can either increase the grip at the rear or reduce the grip at the front. In on-road racing a touring car will oversteer if the rear wing is changed for one with less downforce, since there'll be less effect on the rear of the car.

Pack – The rate at which a shock absorber piston reacts to any quick, sharp movements from the suspension. Fewer or smaller holes in the piston have the effect of slowing down the reaction and the shock absorber is said to have more pack. This is used as a tuning feature, as it can help to reduce the impact when the car lands from jumps or travels through a series of medium to large jumps. Generally, you'd use less pack on a bumpy track and more on one with large jumps that result in heavy landings.

Pan car – An American phrase used to describe a rear-wheel-drive on-road car that uses a chassis made from a flat 'pan' of graphite, carbon fibre or fibreglass. These specialised circuit cars are extremely fast but require a very smooth tarmac or carpet surface to race on.

Peak detect – This is the most popular charging method, where the fast charger detects that the pack has reached its peak voltage and switches off the charging process. To do this the charger continuously monitors the overall pack voltage and actually stops charging once the pack begins to be overcharged, when instead of going up the voltage drops. A fully charged battery will always be warm to the touch, this heat being created by the charge rate (Amps) or the level of overcharge. On most modern-day competition-spec chargers this is adjustable.

Pinion – The small gear fitted to the end of an electric motor. The more teeth on the pinion, the higher the top speed of the car will be, but at the expense of acceleration and battery duration. There's also a pinion gear inside a gearbox where there's a 90° transfer of drive. The term again refers to the smaller of the two, with the larger one on the differential being called the crown gear.

Piston (engine) – In an internal combustion engine the piston fits tightly inside its liner, as this is what creates the compression that in turn creates the heat that allows the fuel/air mixture to ignite. This then drives the piston down and in turn transmits drive through the crankshaft to the car's transmission.

Piston (shock absorber) – This is the part of the shock absorber that passes through the oil. How soft or heavy the damping action feels depends upon the size of the holes in the piston. You can change pistons to adjust a car's handling or use different oils.

Pole position – When you reach the end of qualifying you get to race your final, and if you've come out as the TQ or top qualifier you win 'pole'. When you start from pole you're in the best position, with the other cars all behind you on the staggered grid. The driver in pole has the choice of which side of the grid they want to start from and displays a number '1' sticker on their car.

Pull-start – A recoil system used to quickly turn over a nitro engine and start the combustion process. Modern pull-starts use short cords that are firmly tugged to start the engine. Most entry-level engines come with a pull-start as these are simple and reliable, whereas more expensive kits may include an electric starter or similar feature. Due to the weight incurred with a pull or electric start arrangement, competition engines have neither and utilise a starter box to bump-start the engine using the flywheel.

RIGHT The pull-start system has been around for years and is a simple but very effective way of firing up an engine.

FAR RIGHT The race director is in charge of a meeting and might also be in control of the timing equipment.

Qualifying – The mechanism used to determine the fastest cars at a race meeting. Different qualification methods are used. FTD qualifying sorts the drivers in order of who completed the most laps in the allotted time. Round-by-round qualifying awards points for the finishing order in each round, drivers then being sorted in order of their total points. Round-by-round is used when track conditions are expected to change significantly during a race meeting, since it may prove impossible to complete more laps when the track's badly rutted or soaking wet.

Race director – The official charged with running a race meeting. The race director will call the drivers to the rostrum, make sure the laps are counted accurately and ensure that each driver marshals the race following his own.

Racing line – The fastest route around a racetrack but not necessarily the shortest, as it rarely follows the track's shape. The racing line is a smooth, flowing route that maximises the width of the circuit. It makes the corners less sharp and therefore ensures that cars can achieve the highest possible corner speeds.

Rallycross – The term used to describe a nitro-powered 1:8 scale off-road car. Powered by a 3.5cc nitro engine, these 4WD cars are capable of tackling bumpy terrain at high speeds.

Rich – A situation where a nitro engine is being supplied with too much fuel. The carburettor can be adjusted to allow more or less fuel into the engine. so if it's running rich the main or high-speed needle should be adjusted by turning it clockwise to lean it and restrict the flow. Often an engine that's too rich won't achieve maximum speed and will blow a lot of smoke from the exhaust.

Ride height – The ride height is the distance between the lowest part of the chassis and the ground, and should be set just high enough to allow the suspension to work effectively. If the ride height is set too low the shock absorbers won't be able to soak up the bumps because the chassis will bottom out, whereas too much ride height can result in excessive chassis roll when cornering,

which may cause the car to pick up its inside wheels or even flip over. A car should be run as low as possible without having any adverse effect on the handling.

Roll centres – Points at the front and rear of a car about which the chassis rotates. Drawing a line between them gives the roll axis. The position of the roll centres affects the handling of the car and will be different from kit to kit. Altering the position of the suspension links can change the roll centres.

Rostrum – A raised section of a racetrack where the drivers stand during a race to control their cars. This can vary from track to track, as indoor venues tend to use wooden benches or a stage whereas outdoor tracks tend to have a dedicated rostrum. Having all of the drivers together ensures that each gets a similar view of the racetrack and also minimises radio interference, since your car is only close to the other drivers' radio transmitters when it's also close to your own.

Rotating weight – All the rotating parts on a model car, such as the wheels, driveshafts, bearings, differentials, drivetrain and gears. See page 97.

RTR – Ready-to-run. See page 31.

Saddle pack – Refers to the layout of a battery pack where the cells are arranged in two groups and joined by a piece of wire. This design allows the battery to be positioned where the manufacturer wants the weight.

Scale saloon – An older name for a 1:10 scale touring car. Electric-powered scale saloons are 190mm wide whereas 1:10 nitro-powered saloons are 200mm wide. Both aim to look similar to the cars raced in full-size touring car events.

Schottky diode – A small directional diode that's soldered across the terminals of an electric motor to reduce the arcing that occurs under braking. It's one way to suppress the tiny electrical signals generated by an electric motor that can result in a radio glitch.

Scrutineering – Before or after a race a car has to pass through scrutineering, where race officials called scrutineers will check that the vehicle

FAR LEFT Rallycross cars are exciting to watch, with bundles of power and lots of noise.

LEFT A battery split into two is referred to as a saddle pack.

RIGHT The official scrutineers in action as they check the legality of a car.

FAR RIGHT Correct use and set-up of a slipper clutch will make an RC vehicle easier to drive and reduce wear on components such as tyres.

complies with all the rules with regard to equipment used, dimensions and weights.

Servo horn – A moulded plastic or alloy item that fixes to the output gear of the servo and allows the servo to connect to the steering linkage.

Servo reverse – System enabling the commands on a transmitter to be reversed without having to adjust the fitting of the servos. See page 115.

Servo throw – A servo operates in both directions and it's important that the throw is set to be the same, left to right. On more expensive transmitters you can use the end-point adjustment (EPA) to ensure that this is achieved.

Shock absorber – Fitted to almost every form of RC car, a shock absorber is fitted between the wishbone and the chassis to allow it to ride the bumps. Shock absorbers, or 'shocks', are a tuning tool and can be changed to alter the way a car drives. Whilst most competition-spec kits have one shock per corner, there are other RC models – such as monster trucks – that can have up to ten fitted. See also 'dampers'.

Shock travel – This term describes how much movement a shock has, which can be changed by altering the number of shock travel limiters the absorber has inside it. This reduces the suspension droop or down travel and speeds up the direction change during cornering. On smooth high-grip surfaces such as carpet, adding limiters to reduce the travel will sharpen the handling. Taking limiters out to increase the amount of shock travel will help on bumpy tracks or where there are big jumps.

Silicon oil – This type of oil is used inside shock absorbers and geared differentials. In a shock it slows down the effect of the return spring (on the outside), otherwise the suspension would be very bouncy. Altering the oil viscosity is used to modify the handling over bumps as well as through corners. Using oil also slows down the speed in a geared differential. Lighter oils are better on bumpy tracks and make the car easier to drive, whereas thicker oils work best on flatter, faster tracks.

Skimming – The commutator on a brushed motor wears due to its contact with the brushes and is

returned to perfect condition by being 'skimmed' using a special lathe, which removes the burnt copper material.

Slipper clutch – Fitted to off-road vehicles, a slipper clutch provides a form of traction control that makes the car smoother to drive by taking away some of the initial acceleration. Slipper clutch pads are sandwiched between plates and the amount of slip can be adjusted by loosening or tightening the spring. On slippery tracks you run the slipper clutch looser than on high-grip tracks. The slipper clutch will help stop rear-wheel-drive cars from pulling a wheelie and will save the transmission on 4WD vehicles from getting damaged by the shock and impact when landing from large jumps.

Spring rate – Refers to the stiffness of a set of springs. A soft set will typically increase the traction at that end of the car. Go too soft and the car may be sluggish to respond when entering corners and will roll and pitch excessively under cornering and braking. If the spring rates have to be changed significantly the oil or damper pistons may need to be altered too.

Sprung weight – The weight of the chassis and all the parts mounted on it. These are the bits that bounce up and down on the springs of the car, such as the chassis itself, the shock towers, the radio equipment and the engine. See page 97.

Spur gear – This is the large gear driven by the pinion gear attached to the motor. A smaller spur gear will increase a car's top speed, but at the expense of acceleration. Spur gears are available with different numbers of teeth to allow the gear ratio to be adjusted, as well as different diametrical pitch (DP) depending upon the use and application. The DP of the spur gear has to be the same as that of the pinion.

Stadium truck – 1:10 scale 2WD truck powered by either a nitro engine or an electric motor. They were made famous in the United States and are very popular over there due both to their simplicity and the popularity of trucks in general.

Starter box – Most competition nitro engines rely on a starter box to turn them over, like a bump start. Whereas lower spec or RTR engines come with a pull-start, race-spec examples eliminate the weight of a recoil system by using a starter box. The car locates on the box, and pushing it down makes a connection that spins a rubber wheel inside and bumps it against the engine's flywheel. Turning the engine over for just a few seconds is enough for it to fire.

Steering rate – A transmitter control that enables you to adjust the amount of movement in your steering servo. The normal range of adjustment can be from full down to as little as 20 per cent. See page 115.

Stock motor – Arguably the most popular class of electric racing. A stock motor uses specific components in order to control its cost and performance, which keeps the playing field very level. It has fixed timing, uses bushes rather than bearings, and is made up of a single strand of fixed gauge wire wrapped 27 times around the armature (referred to as a '27x1').

Sub-C – All 1:10 and 1:12 scale electric kits use sub-C sized cells or batteries, which ensures parity between manufacturers. The size refers to the physical dimensions of the cell rather than its capacity.

Temperature gun – Used by nitro racers to test the temperature of their engines. The reading can be used to help tune the engine to achieve the best performance. A nitro engine has an ideal working temperature window: if it gets too hot when the settings are too lean (not enough fuel), performance can become erratic and the life of the engine can be reduced; if the settings are too rich (too much fuel), the engine will never reach its full potential and may again be damaged.

Timing ring – This is part of a modified electric motor and is a removable item that holds the endbell in place. The endbell can be rotated along with the ring so that the timing can be adjusted. More timing (called advance) increases the RPM and the current draw whereas less timing can help make the motor smoother to use. Electric motors always run some degree of advance, indicated on the side of the motor can. You should only reduce the amount of timing within the bounds indicated by the manufacturer.

Titanium – A metal that has a number of benefits over steel or something similar in that it's light and yet strong. Unlike aluminium, titanium has greater strength but is equally as light. For this reason it's used on key areas that take a lot of abuse, such as hinge pins, shock shafts and turnbuckles.

Toe-in/Toe-out – Best looked at when viewed from overhead, a car is described as being toe-in when the forward-most part of the wheel points inwards. With toe-out, the front of the wheel will

point outwards. This is a great tuning tool, as toe-in – either on the front wheels or the rear wheels – increases stability. As you decrease the amount of toe-in the car will feel pointier. Whereas toe-in or out is an option on the front wheels, the rear wheels will always have some element of toe-in, as this generates lots of forward grip under acceleration.

TQ – An acronym for 'top qualifier', meaning the driver who's at the top of the time sheets at the end of each round of qualifying. The TQ when qualifying ends will start the A final from pole position.

Track – Measured from the very outside of one wheel to the opposite side, track affects the stability and handling of a car. A wider track offers greater stability over a narrower one, whereas if you make the front track narrower you can increase the amount of steering.

Transmitter pound – An area set aside for the storage of transmitters when they're not being used. A pound is part and parcel of large race meetings and eliminates the chances of someone accidentally turning their radio on when another race is being run. If that radio is on the same frequency as another there's a good chance that it will cause interference, and cars could go out of control.

Transponder – Available in two forms, either as a handout or a personal item, a transponder unit is fitted to your car before a race and counts your laps as the unit passes over a particular area of the track, called the loop. Each time your car passes over the loop the computer receives a signal and adjusts your race details. Transponder systems are incredibly accurate and measure the laps to within a thousandth of a second.

Trim – Parts of the transmitter located in and around the throttle and steering that allow the car to be set up so that it goes in a perfectly straight line, and ensure that the when the transmitter is left in the neutral position the throttle isn't operating in either forward or reverse modes.

Trued and glued – A term used for foam tyres that are supplied already glued to a set of rims and

ABOVE Truggies have developed from buggies and are fitted with a truck-style body – hence their unusual name.

BELOW An underbody will save the internal electrical components from potential water damage.

have been trued perfectly round and to a set diameter. This allows them to fitted and used immediately after purchase. Doing the job yourself takes time, requires specialist tools, and is also quite messy!

Truggy – The name given to 1:8 scale nitro off-road trucks, derived from the fact that they were converted 1:8 buggies fitted with truck bodyshells.

Turnbuckles – Turnbuckles are fitted instead of threaded rods to connect the suspension or steering. One end has a regular thread while the other has a left-hand thread. This allows for fast adjustments in terms of length if you change the set-up.

Turns – The number of times that the wire is wound round the armature stack of an electric motor. Varying the number of turns of wire on each pole changes the magnetic field strength, so a motor that has a lower number of turns will achieve higher rpm, albeit at the detriment of less torque and higher current draw. Lower performance RC models often come with higher numbers of turns, which make them easier to drive and offers longer run times between recharges. Likewise, the fastest drivers use very low-turn motors to achieve the best on-track performance. See also 'wind'.

Tweak – Term applied to an on-road chassis that may not handle the same when turning left and right.

Two-speed – A system of two different ratios fitted to monster trucks as well as racing cars. The system allows the engine to work on a bigger ratio at first to achieve good acceleration, then at a preset point – normally governed by the rpm of the engine – a centrifugal clutch allows the gear to shift into the lower ratio to provide a high top speed.

UJ or universal joint – A driveshaft featuring UJ linkage allows incredible articulation. Although a dogbone driveshaft (named after its shape) is simpler in design, it isn't of such high quality and can't handle as much movement without risk of falling out in off-road applications. A UJ system also offers better performance due to reduced play in the drivetrain.

Underbody – A moulded Lexan cover used to protect the radio equipment during wet-weather operation. These are very popular on 1:10 scale touring cars that compete in both damp and wet conditions, since touring car bodies don't fit tightly around the chassis and it's easy for water to penetrate and damage expensive electric components such as the speed control.

Understeer – When a car doesn't want to turn into a corner and pushes wide instead – usually because the front tyres aren't generating enough grip – it's described as understeer. Slowing down is often sufficient to make the car turn-in, but to maintain speed round a corner the car's set-up has to be changed by altering the tyres, shock absorbers or weight distribution.

Undertray – Like an underbody, an undertray is used to protect the chassis and its contents from dirt and water. They're fitted to many off-road cars that compete on surfaces such as grass and dirt where there's a lot of spray coming off the tyres. An undertray is normally screwed to the chassis and fits tightly to the bodyshell.

Unsprung weight – The moving suspension parts of a car that move up and down with the wheels, sit underneath the springs, and have to react to all of the lumps and bumps on the track. See page 97.

Viscosity – Term used to describe how thick oil is. Shock oils and diff oils come in a range of different viscosities, and this can be used to tune the handling. Different oils affect how hard or soft the suspension is to push up and down (static damping). Changing the oil will affect how the car performs through a corner from turn-in to mid-corner and exit. The oil also controls the way the car reacts to bumps.

Weight distribution – Most cars are designed to

have 50:50 weight distribution left to right, although this is rarely the case with the front to back balance. If the left-to-right ratio is very different the car won't have the same turning performance from one side to the other. For balanced handling the front-to-rear ratio on both the left-hand and right-hand sides of the car should match the front-to-rear weight distribution of the whole car.

Wheel offset – Offset is measured in millimetres and, depending upon the amount, refers to where the stub axle sits in relation to the centre of the wheel's width. For example, 3mm offset wheels increases the overall width (track) of the car by 6mm. Generally, though, the majority of touring car rims are zero offset.

Wheelbase – The distance between the centre of the front axle and the same point on the rear axle. Most competition cars feature an adjustable wheelbase so that the driver may adjust it to a shorter wheelbase to improve turn-in and acceleration or a longer wheelbase if more stability is needed.

Wind – This is how the performance of a motor is assessed and refers to the number of wires wrapped around each pole of the armature inside the motor. The acceleration, current draw and rpm are all governed by the overall amount of wire used. If two motors use the same wire, a lower wind like a six-turn will have greater RPM than a nine-turn. These motors can also be manufactured in single-, double-, triple- or quad-wind formats. A single-wind has one wire on each pole whereas a quad will have four. See also 'turns'.

Wing – Fitted to the boot area of a touring car, a rear wing is used to create downforce that helps the car to generate grip at high speed. An off-road car uses the same principle to balance the handling and make the car jump better through the air.

World Champion – The ambition of every racer is to be the best in the world. World Championship events take place every two years for the major classes and allow only the very best drivers from each country to take part. These qualify through their National Championship and then go on to represent their country against up to 139 others.

Appendix 2 – The National Association

ABOVE The British Radio Car Association is allied with the full-size Motor Sports Association (MSA).

TOP Joining the BRCA protects you not only as a driver but also as a marshal.

The British Radio Car Association promotes the construction and racing of radio control cars throughout the UK and encourages national and international racing among its members. Formed by the first RC car enthusiasts about 25 years ago to provide a common set of rules for racing, it's now one of the biggest RC associations in the world.

The volunteers who run its various Sections (or racing classes) and form the Executive Committee have a complicated job that requires them to balance their members' needs with the ever-increasing requirements of legislation covering safety and liability. The Executive Committee runs the association, and each Section runs its own affairs, from the National Series to construction and racing rules.

At the time of writing membership costs £14 if you join as an individual, but less if you join through your local club. So, what do you get for less than the price of a pair of wheels and tyres?

One member, one vote

Most importantly, you get the entitlement to suggest changes to the BRCA rules, and to vote on those changes at the association AGM each October. This is an important and vital right, since it means that the members run the BRCA. None of the Section Committees, or the Executive Committee, can make changes to the rules unless the members who attend the AGM agree them.

Insurance

Next, you get public liability insurance that covers you against injury or damage that may be suffered by someone else while you're using your car at a race meeting. It doesn't cover damage to cars and equipment, but if something went wrong and your car hit someone in the crowd you'd have insurance against their claim. Everyone should have this coverage for his or her own peace of mind. It's very easy to sue people these days, and if you can't afford to pay the compensation you could lose a lot more than your racing gear!

Compete at the highest level

Your membership card is a drivers' licence that entitles you to enter the BRCA National and Regional Championships organised by your racing section. Each class of car (1:12, 1:10 Touring Car, 1:10 Off-Road, 1:8 Rallycross, etc – there are now ten BRCA racing classes) organises National or Regional (or both!) race series which allow you to compete for the title of National Champion. From the National Series you can qualify to race at both European and World Championships by paying for the correct racing licence through the BRCA.

The BRCA Nationals are the most prestigious race meetings in the UK. All the factory-sponsored drivers compete in these events, so it's a chance to meet them and ask about their cars and set-ups. Even if you don't make the A Final, watching the best drivers in the UK duel it out in the National Series is an exciting sight. Details of all the National Series meeting dates can be found on the BRCA website at www.brca.org, along with race reports.

Chit-chat

Each year you get six copies of the BRCA's newsletter, *Circuit Chatter*. This gives you details about your

Section, a complete calendar of BRCA events for the year, and the results of the National Championships. There are often other articles about the BRCA, the latest news from the Executive Committee, and inside information on where the BRCA will be holding displays and shows to promote the hobby.

The BRCA also offers reduced rates at Jarvis Group hotels that you can use at any time, as well as reduced subscription rates to the major model magazines through offers in *Circuit Chatter*.

What's next?

How do you get to be part of this great association? Simply go to www.brca.org, click on 'Join the BRCA' to download the membership form, fill it in and send it to the Membership Secretary, and a licence and handbook will follow in due course. Once you receive these you're insured and can race in the Nationals. If you don't have internet access, write to:

BRCA Membership Secretary
PO Box 90
Tiverton
Devon
EX16 6XQ

BELOW Representing your country at an international event is one of the highest accolades you can achieve. Here the BRCA team line up at the opening ceremony at a recent European Championship.

Appendix 3 – Online information

There are many internet websites dedicated to radio control vehicles. These vary from manufacturers' and online shopping sites to clubs, associations and general chat sites. All of them are worth a visit as they'll help you decide which model to buy and give you advice on building it, how to get the best out of it, and where you can go to race it. Here's a selection of our favourite sites and details of what they have to offer.

http://gluk.almipa.com/t-maxx
The largest T-Maxx gallery on the worldwide web, with literally thousands of images of Traxxas's popular truck. You can add images of your own ride here for the whole world to see.

www.beatyourtruck.com
This American site covers everything from Mini-Ts to T-Maxxes and has a large number of cool images of hopped-up trucks. Beat Your Truck also has a section for their own project trucks along with readers' rides, product reviews and a members' forum.

www.brca.org
The British Radio Car Association website offers a wide range of information for the RC racer. Here you'll find race dates and results for most classes of racing and also information on where to find your local club and how to join the association. Although the BRCA is responsible for setting the rules for racing, its main aim is to encourage people to meet up and have fun, and then go racing.

www.buggysport.info
A website that features all the news from the 1:8 off-road rallycross scene, including race news and new product information.

www.cmldistribution.co.uk
The CML website has dedicated areas for planes, boats and cars. It features the latest news, products and competitions from the UK's distributor for Associated, Reedy, Yokomo, Novak and many more.

www.horizonhobby.co.uk
Horizon Hobby UK is the UK importer for lots of products on the nitro scene, from RTR kits to competition on-road racers. You can check out products from the likes of Team Losi, LRP, Peak and Sportwerks amongst others.

www.hpi-europe.com

The European website of HPI Racing provides the latest news from the racing scene and lots more. It provides everything you could want from an RC car website, including details of new products, option parts, accessories, product support and even downloadable wallpaper and video footage.

www.losi.com

All the latest kit releases, team news and set-ups are available on the Losi site, including their incredibly popular Mini-T and Micro-T kits. Since its release, the Mini-T truck has started a boom that's since spread throughout the industry. Their website looks at all the latest parts for the Mini-T through to the massive LST2 and all the nitro trucks in between. There are tips and tyre guides as well as a very interesting section devoted to customers who own Mini-T tracks.

www.neo-buggy.com

This site is dedicated to the rallycross race scene, with lots of news as well as new product releases and race reports. Well worth a regular look for all that's going on around the rallycross world.

www.oople.com

The 1:10 off-road scene is the main focus of this website, and along with a dedicated forum for kits, race meetings and other aspects it's also packed with fantastic action photography from a range of meetings, including the BRCA National Championships.

www.racing-cars.com

Schumacher Racing Products is a UK manufacturer that produces a wide range of cars from 1:10 scale electric tourers right up to huge nitro-powered monster trucks. Like many of the other sites featured here it includes a comprehensive parts list for all their models, but on the Schumacher site you can also download exploded diagrams and full instruction manuals. In addition you can buy spares online.

www.rcracechat.co.uk

This is one of the most popular mainstream forum sites based in the UK and features dedicated areas covering a massive range of topics. The threads are split into sections for electric and nitro-powered models, clubs, regions and classes. The team of moderators on this site is extremely knowledgeable, and with such a large nucleus of users it's a great place to source information and advice.

www.rcracer.com

Radio Control Car Racer is the biggest RC magazine in the UK, with a website that features all the latest race news and dates plus lots of information about clubs in your area and links to the largest RC companies.

www.rcuniverse.com

A US-based website that features all forms of RC including cars, aeroplanes, helicopters and boats, as well as a discussion forum and much more.

www.redrc.net

At Red RC you can find all the latest news from all areas of the sport including news from the racing scene and up-to-date information on car and truck releases, accessories and products.

www.savage-central.com

Savage Central claims to be the largest site on the net dedicated to HPI's Savage truck series. It includes the latest news on these trucks and available option parts, along with forums and member reviews.

www.sgrid.com

Starting Grid is a monthly online magazine aimed at the hardcore racer. In addition to news there are also technical and travel articles available to subscribers, and a huge conference section used by many of the top racers from around the world.

www.teamassociated.com

The multiple World Championship winners show off their speed secrets on this colourful and feature-packed website. There are full details of the company's ever-expanding range of quality RC cars and trucks, plus building hints and tips and downloadable set-up sheets.

www.traxxas.com

Get trucking with the vast range of off-roaders from this bunch of US racers. Since the launch of their extremely successful T-Maxx truck, which has had a huge impact on the RC truck market around the world, Traxxas can do no wrong. Their attractive and easy-to-use website has full details of their entire range. There's also a customer support section and an online chat community.

www.twf8.ws

If you're looking for engine setting and tuning tips then this is the website for you. It's packed with helpful tips and information that'll help you to keep your engine running perfectly no matter what type of car you have.

Appendix 4 – Major distributors

Here is a list of the larger distributors in the UK, along with details of some of the product lines that they represent.

Company	Amerang Ltd
email	enquiries@amerang-group.com
website	www.amerang-group.com
agents for	Hitec, Thunder Tiger

Company	CML Distribution Ltd
email	sales@cmldistribution.co.uk
website	www.cmldistribution.co.uk
agents for	Associated, Checkpoint, HoBao, Novak, Pro-Line, Reedy, Yokomo

Company	Horizon Hobby UK
email	sales@horizonhobby.co.uk
website	www.horizonhobby.co.uk
agents for	Losi, LRP, KO Propo, Novarossi, Peak, Spektrum, Sportwerks

Company	Kyosho UK
email	sales@kyoshoeurope.com
website	www.kyoshoeurope.com
agents for	Kyosho, Sirio

Company	Mirage RC Enterprises
email	sales@mirageracing.com
website	www.mirageracing.com
agents for	Hot Bodies, HPI, Hudy, Nosram, Team Orion, Xray

Company	Ripmax
tel	020 8282 7500
website	www.ripmax.com
agents for	CEN, Futaba, OS, Sanwa, XTM

Company	Schumacher Racing Products
email	Schumacher@racing-cars.com
website	www.racing-cars.com
agents for	Fantom, GM Racing, Schumacher

Company	Spire Model Distribution
email	support@s-m-d.co.uk
website	www.s-m-d.co.uk
agents for	Eureka, GO, Hong Nor

Company	Ted Longshaw Model Cars
email	ted@tedlongshaw.co.uk
website	www.tedlongshaw.co.uk
agents for	Medial Pro, Mugen, Ninja

Company	The Hobby Company
email	sales@hobbyco.net
website	www.hobbyco.net
agents for	Acoms, Carson, Tamiya

Index

Aerials 56-57, 59, 116, 124-125
Aerodynamics 59, 105-106
Air filters 66, 69, 71, 140
Anti-lock brakes 114
Anti-roll bars 76, 101, 141, 157

Batteries 16, 27, 31-32, 52, 54, 79, 88-95,
    113, 134
    AA 10, 33, 54, 79
    computer-matched 89-90
    LiPo 54, 145
    NiCd 88-89
    NiMH 54, 88-89, 137, 145
    on-board 79
    power packs 54, 88-95, 145
    receiver 51, 78-79
    rechargeable 32, 54, 79, 88, 136, 139
    saddle packs 165
    12V 92-93, 118, 133-134, 139
Battery charging 31, 54, 92-94, 118, 139
    discharging 94-95
Belt-drive models 137
Bodyshells 23, 32, 38, 41, 44, 58-63, 66, 68,
    105-106, 143
    Lexan 28, 41, 59, 61, 137, 162
Booth, Phil 14-15
Braking 50-53, 80, 98, 101, 112, 114, 119,
    123, 140
    hydraulic discs 144-145
    regenerative 52
Buggies 9, 16, 27-28, 135, 139, 141-142,
    152, 156, 163, 168

Camber 76, 78, 103
Capacitors 72, 125
Carburettors 53
Centre of gravity 57, 98
Chassis 31, 33, 39, 44, 66, 68-69, 74-76,
    84-85, 96-97, 122, 137, 139, 141,
    143, 157
    balance 42
    carbon fibre 6, 8, 18
    covers 73
    flex 42
    Lexan 29
    set-up 28, 32, 42-44, 50, 84, 86, 95-97,
        100, 138-139
    tweak 74-76
Cleaning 39, 68-74
    after racing 66, 68-71
    electric-powered cars 71-72
    nitro-powered cars 66-71
    unpainted bodyshells 60
    wheels and tyres 45
Clutches 70, 159, 166

Competing 24, 86, 130;
    internationally 19,24, 137

Compressors 68
Cragg, Neil 169

Decals 58, 63
Differentials 44, 67, 77-78, 97, 139,
    141, 160
Downforce 105-106
Drag 106
Drifting 107, 160
Driving techniques 116-119
    back-flips 120
    cornering 118-120, 149
    jumps 27, 117, 120-123, 127,
        139-140, 153
    overtaking 119-120, 130
    practising 117-118, 123, 132, 134, 143
    racing 110, 121
    rostrum position 126
    somersaults 120
    wheelspin 120

Electric motors 86-88, 97, 105, 113, 169
    arcing 125
    brushed 71-72, 86-88, 125, 145
    brushless 71-72, 86, 88, 125, 137,
        145, 158
    upgrading 86-87
Electric-powered models 8, 16, 19, 25-27,
    29, 32, 38, 48, 52, 54, 66-67, 71-73,
    79, 88, 104-105, 113, 125, 130,
    136-137, 139
Engines (see also Two-strokes) 14, 25, 33, 41,
    48-49, 70-71, 97, 139, 167

Four-wheel drive (4WD) 77, 137, 139
Frequencies 22, 115, 126
    27MHz 22, 113-115
    35MHz 115
    40MHz 22, 113-115
    2.4GHz 22, 113, 115-116, 127
    illegal 126
    peg boards 127
    unwanted 72
Four-wheel drive 8, 17, 28, 103, 140, 143,
    156
Fuel bottles 25, 33
Fuel pipes 41
Fuel tanks 69-70, 73, 140-141
    175cc 142

Gearing 103-105, 163
Glow plugs 48, 71, 81, 140, 161

Governing bodies 88, 96
    BRCA 126, 130, 136, 141, 143-144, 153,
        170-171
    IFMAR 89, 136
Grip 101, 106-107, 120, 136, 142, 151, 155

Handling 10, 42, 59, 74, 78, 84-85, 98, 101-
    102, 105-106, 141
    oversteer 163
    roll 98-99, 103, 163
    understeer 106, 169
Hop-up parts 42, 84-85, 135

Infrared control 22
Insurance 123
Internet websites 131-132, 136, 144-145, 153,
    171-173

Japanese coupés 107, 160

Kits 6, 11, 14, 23, 25, 29-33, 36, 49, 67, 121,
    140-141, 143, 163
    assembly techniques 40-41
    building 10-11, 36, 41-42

Local clubs 25-26, 28, 31, 36, 68, 118, 120,
    127, 130-134, 137, 140-141, 144-145, 155
Longshaw, Ted 15-16
Lubrication 41, 66, 71, 101, 160

Magazines 131
Maintenance 10, 23, 66, 80, 84
Model shops 22, 24-25, 28, 31-32, 36, 49,
    59, 131, 145, 153; trackside 132
Motor lathes 39, 72

Nitro fuel 10, 25, 74, 134
Nitro-powered models 8-9, 14, 25-26, 29-30,
    32, 41, 66-71, 79-80, 104, 139-143, 163
    placement of radio gear 51
    starting 48-49, 164

Off-road models 8, 17, 27, 31, 33, 53, 76,
    105, 135, 138-144, 149, 152-153, 155

Paint schemes 32, 41, 58-61, 105, 107, 137
    spraying 38, 58-62
Pit areas 67, 133, 135
Pit lane 153
Pit persons 80-81, 143
Pit stops 80-81, 130, 141
    Pole racing 14
Preston, Dave 15
Protective bags 80
Pull starters 48-49, 164

Race tracks 24-25, 28, 142-143
  Astroturf 139, 155
  carpet 29-30, 78, 136, 139, 150-152
  designing 148-152
  dirt 139, 148
  grass 139, 152, 155
  indoor 26, 136-137, 148, 151-152, 154
  laying out 150-151
  markers 149, 151-152
  marshalling 153, 170
  on-road 27, 30, 153
  off-road 30, 66, 138, 142, 148-149, 152-
  153, 155
  permanent 153
  soaking 155
  tarmac 136, 139, 143
  temporary 122, 148, 152, 155
  walking 118, 134
Races
  European Championship 16, 171
  Monaco 1978 14-15
  Paris Grand Prix 1975 16
  World Championship events 17, 45, 89,
  130, 136, 150, 155, 169
Racing 10-11, 17, 22, 24, 26, 28, 130-145
  back garden 16, 19, 25
  damage 63, 121
  disqualification 100
  drivers' briefings 134
  grid positions 134, 144
  indoors 26, 29-30, 135-137, 139, 148,
  151-152, 154
  in the wet 69, 74
  practice sessions 143
  qualifying 134
  refuelling 80-81, 130, 141
  seeding 130-131
  strategy 143
  technique 121
  tyre changing 80
Racing classes 132, 134-137
  Large scale off-road 144
  Large scale on-road 143-144; Eco 143;
  Four-wheel-drive 143; National 143; Super
  National 143
  Mardave V12 136-137
  Micro 135-136
  Mini-stock 136
  1:5 Bikes 144-145
  1:8 Nitro On-road 142-143
  1:8 Rallycross Buggy 140-142, 165
  1.10 IC 139-140
  1:10 Off-road 139, 149
  1:10 Touring car 137
  1:10 Truck 140-141
  1:12 On-road 136
Radio gear (see also Transmitters and
  Receivers) 50-51, 78-79, 97, 110-116, 143
  crystals 114, 118, 126-127
  Direct Sequencing Spread
    Spectrum 113, 127
  fine-tuning 50
  mounting 57

sealed boxes 73
  steerwheel 111-112
  stick control 110-112
  testing 52-53
Radio interference 73, 113, 124-127
  external signals 126-127
  glitches 124-126
  protection 116
Radio terms 114-115
Rally cars 29
Ready-to-run (RTR) models 10, 18-19, 32-33,
  54, 110, 141
Rear wings 105-106
Receivers 53-54, 57, 72-73, 78-79, 110-112,
  116, 124, 127
  protecting from shocks 127
  voltage 125
Reckward, Daniel 124
Remote control models 22
Ride height 43, 77
Rostrums 126, 134-135, 149, 153-154
Rules and regulations 14, 86, 96, 98, 100,
  106, 115, 126, 130, 132, 136, 142
Running costs 30
Run times 32

Scales 23, 29
  1:5 9, 18-19, 31, 130, 143-144
  1:6 31
  1:8 8, 14-17, 23, 26-27, 30, 33, 139,
    141-143, 148
  1:10 7, 16-17, 26-27, 29-30, 43, 136-137,
  139-140, 149, 153
  1:12 16, 29-30, 136
  1:16 130, 135
  1:18 23, 29, 130, 135
  1:36 19, 29
  quarter 143
Schottky diodes 125
Schumacher, Cecil 16
Servos 51, 53, 57, 110-114, 125, 161
  digital 113
  exponential 114-115
  reverse 115
Shaft-drive models 137
Shock absorbers 6, 27, 67, 74-77, 86, 97,
  101-102, 123, 141, 143
Silencers 140
Slot racing 14
Spashett, David 136
Speed controls (ESCs) 52-53, 55, 87-88, 113,
  125, 136, 161-162
Starter boxes 49
Steering 51, 53, 79-80, 110, 112-115, 117,
  119-120, 122, 127
Straight-line check 79-90
Suspension 41-42, 66, 74, 76, 80, 84, 97, 99,
  102, 122, 144, 157
  droop 43, 75
  drop test 42
  independent 141
  settings 75, 100-103
Switches 56, 125

Telemetry 116
Throttles 51-52, 55, 79-80, 87, 110, 112, 117,
  119-123
Timing systems 85
Toe-in/toe-out 76
Tools 36-40, 59, 67, 75, 77, 81, 86,
  90-91, 134
  measuring 74, 85, 100, 103
Touring cars 7-8, 17-18, 22, 28, 30, 43, 76,
  78, 105, 136-137, 139, 162
Toy cars 6, 22-23
Transmission 49
  geared 27
  multi-speed 140
  two-speed gearbox 30, 139, 142
Transmitters (see also Radio gear) 10, 22-23,
  33, 50, 53, 78-80, 110-111, 115-116,
  127, 135
  EPA (end-point adjustment) 80, 114
  model memory 115
  problems 126
Trucks 8, 27, 140, 168
  monster 135
  stadium 135
  twin-engined 27
Truggies 9, 27, 141-142, 168
Tweak station 75
Two-stroke engines 9, 18-19, 31, 130,
  143-144
Tyres 44-48, 75-76, 78, 80-81, 84, 97-100,
  103, 106-107, 140, 142-143, 151-152,
  155, 166
  checking 78
  contact patch 100-101
  foam 78, 136, 139-140, 152, 155
  gluing 44-47, 78, 159
  low profile 103
  pre-glued 48
  silicone-coated 29
  soft racing 155
  truing 78

Vibration 40, 127

Waterproofing 73-74, 168
Weight 96-97
  distribution 42, 74, 95, 100, 123, 137
  minimum 98
  rotating 97
  saving 96-97
  sprung 97-98
  transfer 98-99, 101
  unsprung 97-98
Wheelarches 60
Wheels 44-47, 78, 97, 106-107, 113, 142
  chrome 107
Wiring 55-57, 124
  checks 80
  receiver leads 55, 125
  unreliable connections 124-125